Knee Reading 101

Madame Genu

ii

Cover design created by

Original artwork by Justin K. Carter

ISBN 978-1-4357-1188-4

Copyright © 2008

Printed in the USA

Second Edition ♥

http://stores.lulu.com/knees

Someday as I do now and then, I'll pick a book by you...
-Gordon

"Wow! It's ingenKNEEous-"
-Micky Hades

DEDICATED TO: Jungle Cub Super Hero extraordinaire, my truly amazing dad, Gano the brave one, Slater a most devilish muse, little Miss Leiker with her Hush Puppy shoes and of course Houdini.

iv

SPECIAL ACKNOWLEDGEMENT to Gypsy as well as all the heart-warming souls that openly shared their knees, secrets and spirit.

FORWORD-

Choosing to venture the world with Madame Genu, you're apt to share specific traits. Actually liking people, enjoying their company and finding the quirks intriguing makes it easy for you to be a good listener. Those rose-colored specs you sometimes wear are merely tinted not distorted. You can still see things including yourself for what they really are. No credit is preferable to discredit or having the integrity of your intentions questioned. You hold education in the highest regard. Always ready to investigate the abstract with a sharp mental grasp clearly rendering you a potent candidate for teaching. Though one may not be religious per se, there is a deep spirituality present. Influenced by the Yin and Yang of life is a duality of being expressed partly in public performance which is quite different then your private profile. A desire for fairness and balance is often reflected in pairs; two passions, TVs, modes of transportation, dogs or cats. Possessing a reasonable respect for authority and free of malice you discern no practical use in physical aggression. Damaging and taking advantage of others isn't a prerequisite for your survival or satisfaction. You tend to be an open-minded inquisitive sort, pure hearted and self-starting who maintains a pleasingly wry sense of humor. Recognizing one's own characteristics in the above description could mean having found your true calling!

Inspired by true events and real people-

CONTENTS

Once upon a knee...

Somewhere amidst a sexual revolution and women's lib a vivacious enterprising young mother found herself divorced then tossed into the 'what's your sign' single scene. It was disappointing reruns of adolescent mixers, different players same cat and mouse games. Male trappings and turfs still dominated. Frustrated she literally bellied up to the bar and dared to become Gypsy Rose Knee. It was an artiste's grand opening into character divination utilizing features of the knee as an oracle. By 1974 her reign had flourished: the talent perfected, designing knee motif jewelry in addition to scarves (tie-dye/batik?), and then writing 'Gypsy's Basic Knee Reader'.

Approximately fifteen years later, this freelance magician stumbled upon a second hand edition. During the five stoplights home, I managed to feverishly skim it like a comic, two pages at a time. The resulting adrenaline rush was electrifying! One could not help but identify with Gypsy, her attitude and formula were astonishingly similar to my own while turning 21 in college. We will browse those days for a better understanding to what extent the connection existed.

§

On entering bars or clubs the invariable junior high tribal structure ruled, girls clustered while boys sized up their prospects. Not to forget the last call 'anyone will do' panic! Sweet young thing or not, how on earth could one weed through a venue that had expanded ten fold? What if Mr. Right was just five feet away? It was more than competition -time as well as resources were limited and this poor student had to come up with a plan! Project 'meet cute guys' started by compiling simple yes or no benign questions disguised as

a school assignment. Yes folks those hard earned
educational dollars put to use!

A neighbor, coaxed by her theatrical fantasies was
convinced to shadow in a little experiment. Safety in
numbers, emotional support plus she undoubtedly would
have taken notice of my fluttering about. On a mission
armed with clipboards, we would approach opposite sides,
working inward, and surveyed one person per table checking
off a bogus tally sheet. This enabled a broader sweep of the
room while giving a full view to elevate curiosity. Meanwhile it allowed for polite exits and golden opportunities to
hook up other singles. Keeping our guise intact everyone
was considered valuable. Though it was often strange with
couples, the observing mate would be concerned about
something they had not been previously privy to. Of course,
they never had asked.

These ridiculous inquiries were strategically scripted to
draw out pertinent info on our targets. The below sample
demonstrates the scope and hidden agenda.

ADVENTURES IN HUMAN NATURE
SOCIOLOGY 101

Have you ever run away from home?
  (Were they a good or bad kid? Did they come from a stable
  home?)

Do you leave your living room curtains open all day?
  (Are you secretive, reclusive, lazy or messy?)

Would you ever fly a kite off a ferryboat?
  (Are you adventuresome or stuffy?)

Do your socks match?
  (Duh? Pet peeve.)

Would you ever blown bubbles off the Space Needle?
(Another search for a fun-loving sort.)

Have you ever hit someone of the opposite sex?
(Oddly men openly had 3 very tell-tale answers; they would never
hit a woman, it only happened once or if they deserved it.
Wow a total no-brainer!)

Do you still have your childhood Teddy Bear?
(The world of stuffed critters wasn't limited to bears. It was
found the majority of bunnies, dogs, alligators and teddies
reside in a parent's storage box or attic. When it came to
those that didn't survive the stories where so disturbing the
question had to be removed.)

Do you take your lunch to work or walk?
(Just to see if they're paying attention.)

Did you ever take swimming lessons?
(We're surrounded by water in the Northwest. It's good to
know if someone fears water and how they've chosen to
deal with it.)

Do you know how your parents met?
(It is rather startling how many people haven't a clue!)

Can you touch you toes straight legged?
(Do they voluntarily prove their stuff?)

Did you ever go to camp?
(Playing well with others and teamwork.)

Did you ever meet the Easter Bunny?
(Acquire some religious beliefs.)

Have you ever fallen off a roof?
(Are you accident-prone or a daredevil?)

Can you curl your tongue?
  (Interest was in the willingness to perform a demonstration.)

There was method to the madness and an unmistakable theme: you, you, you, and oh yes, you. No wonder there was a constant outpour of participation, what could be more interesting then them? It was always a marvel how intently we were deemed irresistible and fascinating. Must of been the winning combination; damsels in distress, youthful invincibility, and a spectacular conversational topic.

Acquiring friends along the way by crossing barriers we didn't know existed. There were unexpected gratuities to enjoy; waived cover charges, endless invitations, job offers, food and drinks. All it took was an earnest plea for a quick moment's help. In retrospect, this could have been a precursor to speed dating and we definitely were vintage forerunners of wing women. As the semester ended, we moved on to bigger and better endeavors. Little did one know history intended to repeat itself and lessons of the human condition learn here would forever be significant.

§

Let's revisit Gypsy's realm and the beginning of Madame Genu's. Basically, a modified version of Knee Reading was launched as performance filler-it snowballed! Rapidly picking up momentum as magical cohorts tagged me with 'Knees', which stuck like a barnacle. At least it had that single name star quality! (Elvis, Sting, Bono)

Already knee deep into readings before it was realized Gypsy's material had been printed and rolled out of my hometown. How could that have been overlooked? Was it anxiousness or a head in the clouds? Immediately a letter was mailed to 'Patella Publishing', which was returned to sender with no forwarding address. Investigation concluded her book had been progressively self-published and privately distributed. Despite the dead end, instinct kept whispering she was near ergo a search ensued.

For months hundreds of booking agents, promoters, attorneys, entertainers, artists, metaphysical practitioners, new age wannabes, kooks and wacky dos were contacted in pursuit of Gypsy. Each interaction was stranger than the last. It took ricocheting across unfathomable obstacles and following rumors to melodramas before a relative's phone number surfaced. Finally landing at a recorder then leaving an impromptu campy message, there was no more to do but sigh and wait.

That very evening she called. Hallelujah! The sultry voice heard was intoxicating "This is Gypsy". How and why she was found started a congenial dialog. One could tell her reserved blasé demeanor masked uncertainties. Remember I too had procured a knack for successfully reading people and gaining their trust. Carefully curtailing my enthusiasm an admiration and appreciation for her ingenuity was revealed. Meanwhile uncovering striking commonalities triggered Gypsy's maternal heart.

She's proudly Greek, a grandmother, retired and living a secluded life with her two sheep dogs. Apparently, Gypsy had been quite a local celebrity. Frequenting the downtown Hilton where all of the top sports figures hung out. Rubbing elbows in addition to knees with the rich and famous. This mesmerizing lady graciously shared, nurtured and selflessly encouraged. We parted on friendly terms, kindred spirits, anticipating a future meeting. An opportunity to study at the knee of Gypsy Rose Knee-score!

Finding gypsy was so bizarre as well as exhilarating it became the favored 'boy' story- (Narrative that keeps a guy's attention to the very end. There are elements of danger, adventure, mystery, intrigue, and treasure. This is without making mention of sports, cars, sex, food or them.) A juvenile rendition of seeking gypsy was condensed into an article published 1991 by Genii-the international conjurers' magazine. Whoosh-validation from peers!

Sadly wrath of an older sibling stifled any further attempt to hook up or communicate with Gypsy. Admittedly, there's a severe case of Big Brotherism looming here. In defense, he was considered a King among saboteurs and had never been supportive or interested in my passion for magic. I know boo-hoo. Eventually there was conditional tolerance when command performances proved advantageous to his social standing. As such, one could accurately predict he'd rush to judgement and declare Knee Reading distasteful or an embarrassment. To avoid the static I just didn't bother to tell him. Yes, he finally caught wind and the confrontation turned ugly. It was a cruel insulting attack, encompassing harsh accusations of stocking and tormenting some poor woman. What? If the aim was humiliation it worked, there would be no more imposing on Gypsy. The point; Madame Genu foolishly permitted family dynamics to soil and stomp her tail feathers. Thankfully, Knee Reading itself escaped the nasty tirade and survived in splendor. Indeed, it blossomed into a very sweet life.

One would be remiss allowing Knee Reading to get lost, fade away, go by the wayside or not pay proper homage to a brilliant predecessor. Gypsy originally concocted Genuology as a lark. She gave carte blanche in hopes others would create their own bliss. It became her ticket to the upper echelon, breaking of bread, fine wine and a few traveling coins. For Madame Genu it was priceless-let destiny and the legacy march on!

THE KNEES PLEASE

Technology is excelling with an astronomical force providing endless opportunities to broaden our horizons. Innovative equipment and gadgets abound. Online one is capable of doing anything: go Green or Blue, run a business, buy, sell, trade, bank, research interest, take educational courses, correspond worldwide, broadcast, movies, music, anonymously host Flash Mobs and You Tube to fame. It's incredible how all of this can be achieved in the comfort of your own bedroom and pajamas. However there is an unmistakable downside to a click and serve existence-an obscure solitude. Many spend more time facing a computer rather than their significant others. Certainly lonely detachment is not a healthy component of life.

Knee Reading is an entertaining antidote for that isolation, a tender art consoling skin starved souls with real human contact. Briefly quenching the forlorn thirst is a potent drug, definitely a better tonic than ever imaged. As a tantalizing countermeasure, it offers non-threatening intimacy and amusement.

Initially there's confusion-what's a Knee Reader? Are you a Palmist, Fortuneteller? Inquiring minds want to know! Privately there is a cheap thrill equating it to Phrenology, probably because of the vain ability to pronounce and spell it. This 1800's pseudoscience of deciphering traits in head bumps is a palatable reference to the majority.

Once they link it with distinguishing character through features of the patella you're confronted with dumbfounded-ness or hoop lowing. Cat calls galore, wolf whistles, a little chicka-chicka boom-boom, cheesy tongue clicks, racy innuendos, stripper jabs, and silly men at the bar attempting can-can kicks with one pant leg rolled up. Madame Genu herself has been guilty of a few flirtatious double-entendres and some ardent teasing (no taunting). Worries tend to diminish in the carefree atmosphere of merriment, laughter and lively banter. Winsomely it's on the endearing side of seduction, promising an intoxicating experience. Graced by your tranquil buffer their guards are let down and the lure of curiosity out weighs fear of an audience. Inhibitions freed, before people are the wiser someone is purely enchanted and primed to be center stage.

In short order you will find adult knees are ignored and have gotten a bum rap, literally. 'Check out that set of knobs' definitely isn't referring to knees. They are not an attribute construction workers ogle at. In fact, fashion designer Halston made disparaging remarks on a TV appearance in the mid-seventies. "If he could remove only one part of a women's body, it would be her knees." Ouch! How rude. Taking exception are Scottish flavored Celtic fest or fairs they have a befitting tradition. Tanked kilt clad men compete in a touchy feely contest to crown the 'Bonniest' or 'Knobbiest' knees. It is women of the Haggis Singers that joyfully fondle and choose a 'King'. Sounds like my kind of party maybe I'll be asked to participate as an honorary judge someday. Upon further inspection, it occurred perhaps these lads were merely humored to grandeur. Hum...

Generally, males are utilitarian viewing knees as a functioning tool. Needless to say, females fixate negatively on any body part mentioned. Inadvertently knees are mistreated, abused, and taken for granted unless of course there's painful damage due to injury or illness.

You'll also be elated as well as relieved to discover how knees enjoy the refreshing breeze of exposure, totally love attention, crave limelight, maintain composure and yearn for a gentle touch. They have a precious unplugged purity that is what makes them so special.

PUTTING ON THE RITZ

To be on this stage one must first take stock of the main elements required: confidence, appearance and mindset. All three aspiring to an incredible place beyond assurance yet shy of brassy. Supporting a state of being where you're calm, cool, collected, detached but not distracted. Moxie!

Building self-esteem takes practice and an empowerment of knowledge. Examine lots of knees, keeping doing it until you realize they possess an overwhelming fascination. Once hooked you'll happily be a knee junkie forever. Next, goof around with friends or family to get your bearings. Center yourself in a quiet meditative moment or take a few deep cleansing breaths. If need be a good old-fashioned internal pep talk helps.

Remember Knee Reading is a unique sport, so there are no preconceived notions and it is very unlikely you'll ever come across competition. Your game; you control the ball, rules, pick and field players while keeping score. In other words, it is always your call! This really should be the bottom line, trumping any and all concerns. It's what sealed Madame Genu's fate!

§

TIP #1-THE GLASS IS HALF-FULL
It has long been established that when entering a room or situation 50% of the people will register you in a positive accepting light. Typically, the balance will be dismissing or negative. As a topical behavior, it can easily be swayed in your favor. This means one can consider a large percentage is already on your side even before any cutes or charm have come into play. That's pretty good odds!

TIP #2-SMILING WITH YOUR EYES
This is an effective way to convey safety and security using
your own body language.

Have 3 head shot photos taken. With a digital camera and
computer access, you can do this yourself. Make sure
you're sitting up and the shoulders are squared.

Photo #1: a big happy smile with teeth and all.

Photo #2: a closed mouth smile.

Photo #3: smile with your eyes, without involving your
                 mouth think of something that melts your heart.
                 Let those loving fluffy feelings emanate through
                 your eyes.

You can see for yourself the third picture projects an
atmosphere of soft welcoming warmth. Albeit feasible opt
for the abeyance of dimmed lighting or candles, dilated
pupils have a similar alluring appeal. Both can put
participants at ease and allow for a trusting comfort zone.

§

     You've heard the buzz before 'dress for success' or was
that 'dress to impress'? In either case both turn out to be
true, clothes can make the man (woman). Physical attraction
seems superficial but it is part of our biological encoding.
The way one presents and feels about themselves has much
to do with how others will perceive them. Many subjects
that are drawn in by appearances dearly want to gain your
approval as well!

So wow folks with your very own brand of stunning eye candy! Identify your style; chatty, perky, sensitive, saucy, sophisticated, mysterious, empathetic, humorous or perhaps there's already an alter ego anxiously waiting. Whatever persona emerges it should be congruent with your attire and respectful to the setting. 'When in Rome…' is an appropriate adage. Blue jeans for a formal reception or a cocktail dress at an outdoor picnic are unbecoming matches. This isn't the manner in which you desire to stand out. You're searching for a flare of costuming that defines your character while classifying the intended role.

§

Your hands are magnificent tools of the trade. Keep them soft and supple-a tender touch can act like a two-way conductor transmitting currents of energy. Remember this is an up close and personal connection. Elaborately embellished manicures are gorgeous yet they can have a predatory over tone and be very distracting. Light plain colors give nails a longer streamline look. Better yet just natural buffing, bringing out a great healthy high gloss sheen. For quick shine, rub your bare fingernails rapidly along the opposite palm's oil crease and fatty pad. FYI: You can always tell the age of woman by her hands.

§

A nose knows the chemistry and influence of aromas. No need to remind you about showering or how a Lysol antiseptic mouth is just as offensive as halitosis. Though when wearing colognes-go easy. Completely avoid combining strong scented deodorants, fabric softeners, perfumes and hairsprays. Eye watering fragrances linger, permeate clothing and irritate. Subtle and seductive is welcome here. Dab on hints of a pheromone or musk product to enhance your mystery. FYI: Blowing into cupped palms to check for bad breath is not reliable. Try licking a small spot on the back of your hand or wrist. Allow to air dry then take a sniff. Kind of gross but it works.

§

Make an effort to determine what suits and accentuates your assets packaging does sell the product. When you've completed the right image quit fussing. Constantly brushing hair out of the way or tugging at a skirt is annoying and makes everyone uneasy. Whether dealing with small gatherings, demonstrating in lecture halls or entertaining the military troops, hygiene and perfected grooming is mandatory.

Mastering one's success as a Knee Reader is a serious commitment. It includes a mixture of guts, perseverance, and maintaining balance. Together they mold a solid platform for your inner strength and creativity. Nobody ever forgets their first kiss, love or Genuologist. An experience of a lifetime let it endure as meaningful, memorable and complimentary to the art. The only secret ingredient is you.

FLOURISHES

Ready to become a 'bonified' Knee Reader, get your razzmatazz on! Maximize the potential it's limited only by your own imagination. Meanwhile serve up a side of self indulgence with these proven gems and nuggets.

Gypsy was big on visual aids gloriously posting an assortment of advertising signs and flyers in the immediate vicinity. A 2-buck tabletop plastic easel or placard is sufficient display space for most. She also made a show of her sophisticated mapping system. Each knee's highlights were recorded on a pre-printed chart. One copy would be autographed for the subject and a carbon retained for her research. This wasn't a route personally tempted finding it time consuming and wanting to avoid a trail of booze stained evidence floating around the parking lot.

Pencils are mini billboards, slogans and numbers-everything is available from camo to classy. Now and then nonchalantly leave one somewhere conspicuous or along side a meal tip. Cheap publicity or just to put an extra little murmur of you into the universe.

Business cards are an inexpenive marketing tool, ideal for networking and recognition. Home computers provide

Exposed

PROFESSIONAL KNEE READING
WITH MADAME GENU

endless options for designing them yourself while still evoking a climate of credibility and intrigue. An attempt to emulate Gypsy with her catch phrase "Knee Reading by Invitation Only" looked good but it wasn't mine. So before

finally adopting Madam Genu there was a little Rockford
thing going on; constantly toying with words, changing
names and printing at will. There are many alternatives.

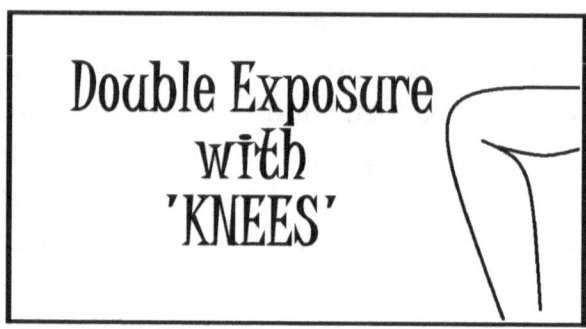

Double Exposure with 'KNEES'

Alas, they were often mistaken for Suburban Hospitality
(hooker), Tart, Fortune Telling or calling cards.

For instance when trying out 'Fan-knee' a girl thought it
would be great for her fiance's birthday. She did call, made
arrangements and sent a check. Awaiting at a sports lounge
were young bucks anticipating a bachelor party's boom box
and stripper. Needless to say they were not the only ones
surprised. Luckily a jovial bunch already three shots to the
wind and very agreeable to knee antics. Despite the
confusion whether deliberate, a trick or her way of kinking
his armor they all had a blast!

Besides time, date and location get the theme. You are
entitled to know the perimeters of a situation and a right to
make rational requests. Detailed directions and a rough map
will alleviate a lot of unnecessary problems or stress. A
simple sketch of the intended layout provides an opportunity
to setup preferred seating positions.

Everyone is into 'freebies', so bee it! An old magic kid
friendly sight gag provides laughs via disposable amusement. Obtain an alphabet 'B' paper punch or pre-made
letters (felt, plastic, whatever). Striped yellow and black
cardstock is most noticeable but any color will do. Keep a

prepared stash on hand and use when needed. You are going for the dual or triple meaning here, once you get the joke it is pretty funny. FYI: Brown construction paper and an 'E' is the recipe for calorie and crumb free brownies. Yum...

Members of bridal (baby) showers are delighted to have yarn or ribbons trimmed in folklore tied above the knee. Elasticized candy or bubble gum necklaces also double as garter souvenirs while marking who has already been read. Yes, the boys like them too.

From serious to humorous and witty, stamps speak volumes. Celebrate the possibilities! Use them as a promotional item. Patrons want your seal of approval; oblige them with an enticing wash-n-wear finale.

YOUR OWN:

THIS KNEE HAS OFFICIALLY BEEN READ
BY MADAME GENU

PROFESSIONAL KNEE READING
WITH
MADAME GENU

DOUBLE EXPOSURE
WITH
'KNEES'

Once upon a knee....

BONIFIED KNEE READING
PARTISAPANT

Too hot to handle!

Rebus (picture words)-

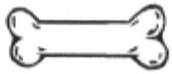

BONE-KNEE

CAR-KNEE

CORN-KNEE

CROW-KNEE

EGG-ON-KNEE

HORN-KNEE

IRON-KNEE

PHONE-KNEE

FAVS-

ANTS IN THEIR PANTS

BEE'S KNEES

BULLS EYE

COOL CHICKS

SMOOCH OR A KISS OFF

TENDER HEARTS & EGOS

100% HOTTIE

TEACHER'S PET!

TOADS TO PRINCES

PIG ON THE KNEE SAFETY AT SEA

18

PHRASES:

All you need is love!

Oooh-la-la!

Kissin & telling

Yadda, yadda, yadda
...blah, blah, blah

...and they lived
happily ever after

The best Is yet
To come!

Just for kicks!

girly girl

If push comes to shove do it yourself:

Draw a reverse motif onto a 2" by 1" artist gum eraser with an ink pen.

Carve out the surrounding areas ¼" deep.

To finish backside adhere moleskin.

PIECE De RÉSISTANCE

Time came when knees obviously had earned a better presentation. Some sort of display stand, a little pomp and circumstance never hurt. The idea of an old-fashioned wood polishing box with a footrest seemed perfect. One could probably be found at a garage or yard sale reasonably priced. Intent here was to refurbish it with a bit of girl glam, maybe a hot pink lining with deco lettering painted on the exterior. Then utilize the brush compartment for cards, ink and stamps

A request to an unassuming neighbor brought much more than a simple stool. This Italian gentleman of hidden bravado had once been employed as a King County private detective for the Pinkerton Investigation Agency. (His credentials proved impeccable.) Apparently, every time an operative left for an assignment they would pass the supervisor's desk next to which was a vintage shoeshine box. Following company policy agents gave their shoes a quick touch up while contemplating the coming task. When the Seattle office relocated, my friend managed to acquire (so to speak) this valet. There is no way of knowing how long Mr. P. I. held it captive before his gracious donation and the resulting rescue.

By removing several cobwebs, piles of dust and wax marks a gorgeous deeply grained solid oak treasure emerged! Any alteration would have just taken away from the richly embedded character. If an inanimate object ever was imprinted with the essence of experiences, it was this box. How fitting to have decades of Pinkerton energy and deductive powers in attendance during Knee Readings. Looking for a pedestal and finding a throne, eureka!

All of these materials can be obtained at dollar, office supply, fabric, discount, warehouse, mercantile, thrift, mail order, eBay, hobby or crafts stores.

Fluff is so much fun it's sweet icing on the cake but truth be told not a necessity. Bear in mind you may end up dining at the White House, stuck in an airport, sunbathing or anywhere. Fortunately, the only equipment required is a knee, your hand and mother wit.

SENSITIVITY TRAINING

Get paper, a pen, this isn't a test and there is no right or wrong answers. Without putting too much thought into it, reply from the top of your head. Briefly jot down four or five things that determine who you are. After waiting five minutes, take a second look. Would you specifically be able to recognize that person?

If you're akin to the majority, you gave cookie cutter responses, a clinical meet-n-greet resume with standard marital, parental or employment stats. These are the topical trappings that outline and frame our structured lives. Nowadays this information is a commodity bought and sold on the open market for calculating probabilities of risk, liabilities, tracking or future possibilities. Government agencies, advertisers, media, developers, researchers, forecasters or apparently any industry involving money will take advantage of the data for financial and directional targeting. Ever felt you were just a number? Bingo!

There's a suspicious association here with pigeonholing which generally carries negative connotations. Looking past but not excluding prejudice or oppression they stemmed from somewhere and still impact social attitudes. Ponder your gauge on these comments; blondes have more fun, accountants are boring, Japanese seem industrious, Chinese appear wise, cartoons are for kids, Blacks fear swimming, politicians lie, Paris is dirty, Mexicans work hard, Jews are shrewd, English humor is dry, teenagers are lazy, it always rains in Seattle, Scotts are thrifty, lawyers are crooks, Swedes are thickskulled, and leopards don't change their spots. Yes, everyone I know has now been offended. Yet comedians and sitcoms thrive on the clichés.

Verily opinions and emotions can even be calibrated by group or mob mentality. An extreme is the current high school scenarios that have rendered a battleground of scarred casualties. Cliques (clicks) have always been painfully evident but these incidents are too drastic for our purposes. We already know whenever folks congregate together a conflict of temperments may arise. The mundane will suffice. Watch the movement of foot traffic and coyness when there's a cute girl distributing food samples. Ever witness a council committee literally sway in the direction of victory? Rocking out at a live concert as the band shifts gears to a ballad, suddenly waves of guys consecutively slip arms around their sweeties. Try to survive the midnight madness etiquette of a 75% off sale!

Statistically speaking stereotypes, countertypes, and subsets are part of our hard wiring and no one or thing is immune. It is a way to simplify complex realities and classify our beliefs. We unconsciously cater to this behavior and are prone to patterned assumptions. Incorporating the commonalities can go a long way in understanding people and their placement. There is a myriad of info to use available through the internet, surveys, books especially sciences of the mind literature, metaphysics, geographic, political and census polls. You're sure to find a connection between labels, order and control that allocate many facets of who we are.

In a Hindu fable, six blind adult males were escorted on an excursion to see the mysterious elephant. Returning they were summoned to share their views and impressions of the animal. Individually they had very distinct recollections and compared it to; a massive wall, long rope, huge serpent, loose fan, mighty tree trunk and a strong spear. Each was more adamant than the next that their concept was correct. This baffled the intelligent men and made them abruptly argumentative. A moral of the story implies it was all a matter of perception. With compromised faculties and a limited vantage point, recognizing the entire picture was impossible.

Applying this analogy to Knee Reading would suggest all of the senses must be engaged for success. Ours are dulled from excessive stimuli and require a reboot refresher course. Manipulate surroundings so as to explore them separately. Focusing on one function at a time provides an opportunity to generate a new respect and awareness. Consider it isometrics for your receptors.

Pay close attention to reactions since these are for your benefit. Although with some, it is nice to have a love or friend around who's got your back.

There is a multitude of sensory recall and physiological illusions that tease our mechanics. Immerse your hand in icy cold water, the other in hot then together in lukewarm. The later will feel both hot and cold.

To challenge taste buds remove moisture from your tongue with a paper towel. Absence of saliva should negate flavor. After every sampling of salt, sugar or other hardtack wash out mouth and repeat the drying.

Manufacturers of edibles inject dyes to influence the appeal of merchandise. Separate avocado dip into two bowls; mix a few drops of green food coloring into one of them. Tell a buddy you're trying out a new recipe and their opinion would be appreciated. Surprise, surprise they favor the implied zest and density of the doctored guacamole.

Nearly everyone can be drug down to the darkness of dismal storms or uplifted by a sunny day. We respond to colors in much the same way. Hospitals as well as prisons cover their walls in placid neutrals, nurseries are blanketed in bright cheer, blacked out windows scream keep out, and we cocoon in tones depicting ourselves.

Language laced attitudes are brushed from the palette and have a motley side too:

<u>COLOR CODED IDIOMS</u>

BLACK AND BLUE-BRUISED
BLACK AND WHITE-CLEAR CUT
BLACKMAIL-EXTORTION
BLACK SHEEP-OUTCAST
BLACK TIE-FORMAL
BLACKBALL-EXCLUDE
BLUE BLOOD-REGAL
BLUE COLLAR-LABORERS
BLUE FUNK-VERY DEPRESSED
BLUE MOVIES-SEXUALLY EXPLICIT
BLUE RIBBON-FIRST RATE
OUT OF THE BLUE-UNEXPECTED
SINGING THE BLUES-EXPRESSING SADNESS
BROWN NOSE-A KISS UP
GRAY AREA-UNCLEAR
GRAY MATTER-THE BRAIN
GREEN WITH ENVY-JEALOUS
GREEN-INEXPERIENCED
IN THE PINK-FEELING CHIPPER
PINK COLLAR-FEMALE OFFICE FORCE
TICKLED PINK-DELIGHTED
PINK SLIP-TERMINATION NOTICE
RED FLAG-WARNING
RED HANDED-CAUGHT IN THE ACT
RED HERRING-A MISLEADING CONCEPT
RED HOT-EXCITING
SEEING RED-ANGER
WHITE COLLAR-MANAGEMENT
WHITE ELEPHANT-ODD BALL MISFIT
WHITE AS A GHOST-FRIGHTENED
WHITE LIE-FIB
YELLOW BELLY-A CHICKEN
YELLOW STREAK-COWARDLY

Auras are an atmospheric static we emit. They are said to radiate a luminous field of cascading colors that have been assigned attributes and divulge a person's current state. Remember mood rings?

If curious, you'll be able to find and examine charts in which the rainbow's spectrum is linked to; healing therapies, pearls, birthstones, crystals, flowers (especially roses), eyes, hair, complexions, tween jelly bracelets and national alerts.

Spend a serious afternoon blindfolded. Go pirate-patch an eye. Watch TV with the sound turned off. Beware of Closed Captioning for hearing impaired it's anticlimactic and the translation is not verbatim. Earplugs or headphones will cut through noise. Inform a companion you'll not be speaking for the evening. Movies aren't fair so go to a restaurant. Nix on written notes! Facial expressions, nodding, pointing, the okay sign, thumbs up or down are about all you publicly have to communicate with. Wear a swimmer's nose clip during breakfast. Set up a Pepsi verses Coke comparison. Direct your conversation towards a person while facing another. Pet a cat with gloves. By now, you get the drift. On the flip side over indulge everything! Really go for the gusto. Saturate life with burst of bold hues, soothing smells, exotic music, varied textures, savory cuisines and guilty pleasures!

According to Madame Genu's philosophy, the sixth and most important sense is intuition. An essence inherently inside everybody and chemically driven to work in unison with the rest. Oddly enough, it's been ignored and demoted to a diluted lukewarm 'common sense'.

For instance, getting on an elevator and the only other passenger gives you an uneasy twinge. You wonder but continue instead of exiting. Why? Politeness conditioning, when something makes your skin crawl, stomach tighten and blood rush most don't want their feelings exposed or to

cause an awkward confrontation. Perhaps it starts
innocently as young children are forced to hug n' kiss
strangers goodbye when they obviously do not want to. This
sends conflicting messages that short circuit instinct.

It is difficult explaining how to relearn the knack of trusting ourselves when countless daily occurrences are dismiss-
ed and blown off as coincidence. Begin by acknowledging
the potential then flex your observance muscles. Monitor
the positive hits you make on the football pool, NASCAR or
lottery picks. Actual betting isn't necessary to contemplate
the outcomes. Calculate your accuracy on predicting the
gender of births. Anticipate what the next TV commercial
will be about. Guess the identity of phone callers. Processing
in this manner tweaks radar and increases consistency. The
following exercise is a personal favorite that should sharpen
judgement and strengthen belief in your capabilities.
Causally check out names, makes and models of vehicles so
the lingo is slightly familiar. Sit by an eatery window that
overlooks the parking lot. Typically, lunch is shorter and
there's daylight for visibility. As people leave, attempt to
distinguish which car is theirs. If a gent is wearing paint
splattered bib overalls, you can bet he's driving a truck.
Urban cowboys aim towards Ford pickups. Bikers tend to be
tattooed and leather clad. Spotting a Bellevue soccer mom
happens long before she finds her mini van keys. Shoes were
always a big clue. Frequently foretelling the right color of
automobiles was an unexpected encouragement. This made
me a very popular date, mainly because it had to do with guy
stuff. Eventually categories and locations were altered to
broaden the scope. The bonus was becoming proficient at
surmising the inconspicuous aspects of any given situation.
Embrace renovating the conscious relationship between
one's perspective and comprehension. The by products are
exhilarating and gladly heed to your scrutiny.

K NEE READING 101

In whatever encounters we have with others it's their character that automatically affects our understanding of them. These opinions in turn establish merit to levels of value and loyalty. Being able to recognize whose trust is worthy has always been a fundamental need. Besides popularity, possessions, employment or marital status perception is greatly influenced by a person's demeanor, speech, mannerisms, gait, and appearance. Since convictions can be reflected in similar expressions man has structured several organized methods in an attempt to lasso their meanings.

Observation is the key agent in Knee Reading. Anyone can state the obvious yet absolutely black or white interpretations discount a million facets in translation. Scan for details especially contradictions; do things jive, are nails bitten to the quick, is there a wedding ring or tattletale tan line? Rely on your noggin and instincts to fill in the gaps of concessions or compromises. As the quintessential clues continually incorporate them during a reading, however your subject's inventory should be compiled by the time they are seated in front of you.

Be mindful both genders weather a hormonal progression of maturity. Each season of growth brings new priorities and milestones, compounding the intensity of responsibility verses risk. Someone in their twenties is more likely to seek future prospects whereas eighty year olds reassess the past and no longer sweat small stuff.

Men are delectable creatures and the preferred clientele. It stands to reason favoring the opposite sex they never cease to amaze. On the average tightly wound around control issues and hesitant to relinquish anything let alone their sentiments. After a lustrum of experience this Reader has concluded there's a hidden passage into the male psyche. Call it their sweet spot. If you merely brush near the naughty nine year old in a guy, he'll gladly wrap himself around your little finger.

Women run off an emotional set of gears and coping mechanisms. Loving to share they are delightfully cooperative, twice as verbal, openly inquisitive, and hopefully addicted to the 'what if' factor. The possibilities excite their sensibilities. Unless it's the Mrs.'s idea prudently solicit her permission in reading hubby. She will kindly repay you in an allied partnership. Note relatives are born informants and colleagues shameless conspirators.

With such an exclusive relationship it doesn't really matter who is milling around even if you're playing to the gallery. Subjects purposefully enter your 3' personal space merging it with theirs, unconsciously granting consent. A bond is then established through hands on contact. To Tango it takes two. Treat it like a dance of courtship

Feedback is crucial in maneuvering the ebb or flow of a reading, each has a tendency to take on a diverse air of its' own, adapt and conform accordingly. It is a waste of time over thinking or second-guessing yourself thus travel the path of least resistance. If negativity is detected, one can make an immediate shift without clumsy backpedaling. Nods are givens whereas shaking the head yes and saying no is a case of 'actions speak louder than words'. Plenty of indicators manifest in minute responses. Tensing or slacking of muscles particularly at the jaw line, furrowing of brows, rocking, leaning forward, arms crossed, pulling away, random fidgeting or a rigid posture. The proximity allows one to ride the wave of their breathing. Is it labored with a whistle, raspy from smoking, shallow, heavy or rapid?

Enjoy the peculiar roller coaster of getting acquainted. It's a guarantee that there's always more than meets the eye.

No worries after a few readings your sensors are tuned up and turned on. Listen to the voice texture, accents and emote rhythms are a telling source:

1. ANGER-increases in shrillness, density and volume.
2. DEFEAT-lackadaisical or a sluggish monotone.
3. EXCITEMENT-rushed staccato speech with pitch alterations.
4. SARCASM-rising and falling tone inflections. Sing-song.

Before comprehending logistics of distance, going right or to the left your parents might have played a Hot & Cold game. Temperature directives are given to pursue a prize. 'Warmer' is encouragingly chanted as one nears the objective and 'Cold' shouted when moving away. Hit the goal and hear congratulatory cheers of you're 'HOT'!

Then again how about Marco–Polo? Subjects will constantly be sending out hints to guide you and our training shows they don't have to be audio. Respect the signals! In a blink, kids can even cite the warnings of traffic lights:

RED-STOP
YELLOW-YIELD
GREEN-GO

Parlay these conceptual principles toward Knee Reading. Diagnose an identity by gathering and compartmentalization of the specifics then consult your internal FBI Profiler.

NUANCES-THE FINE PRINT

It is imperative to set the record straight you're not a
Fortune Teller, which amounts to petty larceny in many
places. Just casually mention your repertoire doesn't
include jail. Going by way of signed waivers leans towards
excessive but could be done. In any case make it perfectly
clear should either of you at any time become uncomfortable
that it is okay to stop-no repercussions!

There was only one incident when a person took the offer
to heart. It was a shi-shi cocktail party where everybody had
swanky jobs. Midstream a sharp dressed man abruptly
threw up his arms in disgust and bailed. Startled the first
inclination was to shrug as he stormed off mumbling
'bullshit'. Another fellow immediately slid into the chair
chanting 'my turn, my turn' which left no hope for damage
control. Regardless the show did have to go on! Mr. Grouch
must have stewed for an hour before discreetly singling me
out profusely apologizing. Confessing terrible embarrassment of how close the reading was then inquiring about
having dinner with him, go figure. (If per chance insulted or
frazzled, get over it to preserve the offender's dignity as well
as your own.) Relax pitfalls are few and far between.

Take it in stride if the subject denies a comment, how a
person pictures themselves is often totally different then the
way others do. You could cast the variables for a
connection since it's going to pertain to them on some level
anyway. But this isn't a debate, contest or fishing derby so
you need to slow the roll before they get adamant. Weaken
and bypass the thought by attaching it to or highlighting
another trait. Gracefully merge into the next area or mute
the ripple with a shrug. If they persist 'you protest too much
my dear' or 'don't shoot the messenger' usually serve as
neutralizing razzes.

You're sure to come across those bent on blowing your cool. Don't bother rising to the challenge. When it comes to hecklers, skeptics or drunks they're a dime a dozen and usually will make no difference. Management, barkeeps, other participants or guest will feel that they are infringed upon, get defensive and come to your rescue.

Should you get a tenacious self-anointed assistant don't panic, make them work for the privilege. Send them on a step n' fetch task; moving chairs, passing out cards, or getting you refreshments. If they continually try to manipulate your time, assign 'Knee Twirling' duty.

THE KNEE TWIRL

Once is not enough-if you try this ridiculous knee trick you will find it irresistible:

1. While seated lift your right foot off the floor and make clockwise circles from the knee down.
2. Meanwhile draw the number '6' in the air with your right hand.

Instantly your foot changes direction. No matter how many times you try to outsmart the knee swirl it always wins. There are a few variations but most people are right sided and this version is more discretely comfortable. Although if you're looking for mayhem get some willing volunteers started out doing the same thing in a standing position. This is so mind boggling you can use it as a great opening ice-breaker, buffer between readings or a way to have kids occupy themselves.

Numerous coordinators of school bazaars, fairs, benefits and stressed parents requested Knee Reading for their events. It's an educated preference to not do kids; since they're not fully-grown declining is justified. If pressed a boring commentary on lack of development is a reliable deterrent. Trespassing is the real reason, children's mental veneers are so fragile and susceptible a fleeting comment can resonate forever-subtly shifting dreams. Adults supposedly have tougher hides and stronger constitutions. Let your conscious be the guide.

It's a matter of prerogative when it comes to reading knees through nylons. For Madame Genu it's preposterous you wouldn't expect a palm reader to decipher through gloves or an oven mitt. This choice has lent to bathroom visits with insistent females laying in wait their pantyhose at varying degrees of removal. Then there was the gal wanting desperately to be involved but was troubled about hairy legs. Instead of pulling up her slacks, she partially dropped them professing only shaving to the knees anyway. Fortunately, it had been laundry day and she was wearing a bathing suit bottom. If only there were more like the bombshell banker playing it up while flooring everyone as she unfastened a garter and seductively rolled down her stocking in a steamy knee tease. Ah, again little girls count on their fingers and big girls count on their legs!

Mini-packs of supercilious 'mean' girls are predictably arrogant, insecure, shallow and vain. Tackle the Queen Bee first, her obedient drones will follow suite. Flattery is the smoking gun of your arsenal. Making sure that it is genuine, spotting a phony is easy and faking compliments or sincerity will ruin your sterling reputation.

Lay stake to your caliber. Openly though modestly claim an accuracy of 97%. Statistics are an assurance to capability and authenticity. Nevertheless, when forced to mingle nip it in the bud if too much information is volunteered. Detour their input, sidestep them or talk about yourself. Breathe easy and have complete faith no one will be able to dispute your credentials, plus you left a 3% loophole.

Although you are not a physician or therapist the position still holds an oath of 'do no harm'. This is by authority of the Karma Police and should not be taken lightly. While fondling knees you are treading in people's heads. If you're dealing with a seriously troubled sort it may warrant a subtle suggestion for professional help. This type of compassion can't be reiterated enough-"Nobody expects the Spanish Inquisition!" So don't do it-there's no reward in haranguing, chastising, belittling or backing anyone into a defenseless corner. Nothing sours folks faster than a feeling they're being judged. They can handle their faults as long as they're cushioned (sugar coated) and it isn't a character assassination. In this business you have to like people and care enough to be considerate. Though there are temptations your good stewardship can afford to be generous!

CHANCE ENCOUNTERS

Acknowledge laws of probability and that on the rarest of occasions a random impulse may surface. If so, it will be out of context with no meaning to you. These are those thoughts or ideas that persistently cross your mind, so insistent as to interrupt your concentration and reading. Pass them on enlisting the subject to make a connection.

Jacky was a tailored sixty-ish woman whose introduction didn't quite fit or gel. Pause was taken to explain the tugging at my brain was so hard I could not get past her name. Flabbergasted she nostalgically testified to a strict upbringing and attending Catholic girls' school. In first grade each student except for Marie, shared a common christening rite. The instructing Sister had gotten frustrated with too many 'Marys' hence the giggling six year olds were lined up and reassigned. Mary Louise became Louise, Mary Margaret-Margaret, Mary Elizabeth-Elizabeth, Beth, Liz, Kay, Kate, Cathy, and so forth. When it came to a fifth Mary Katherine, the appropriate alternates had been used and she was granted permission to make her own prompt choice AKA: Jacky. The entire group of young ladies remained together up to graduation; so ingrained she never changed it back. Was that a 'Hail Mary' or what?

It had been a Seattle kind of day, little cotton puffs scattered against a vibrant background. The breathtaking beauty had permeated everyone's mood except one brash jean clad figure. He slammed himself down snidely grunting, "I suppose you're going to tell me I need to get married and have lots of babies." In that blink, there was a mental burst of cherubs peeking out from behind wisp of white. The thought made me smile and automatically respond to assure him fortunes were not my forte. However, throwing caution to the wind vivid skies of azure and flickering angels were briefly mentioned. This caused his coarse demeanor to immediately soften. Apparently, all he heard was Blue Angels, the squadron this pilot flew with.

An effort was made to ignore images of crystal, certainly a purchase of flee market wine goblets hours earlier was seeding the moment. It was pointless, stemware kept clouding concentration. Addressing this issue with the burly dude was strange but necessary. Stupefied and without hesitation he admitted having a rental storage unit, deliberately concealed for years packed with Princess House.

"Darling you look like a young, ah, you know, ooh what's that big blue fish that people mount on trophy walls? Um, his best buddy was the slim guy on Hollywood Squares, ah ha, Wally Cox!" Absolutely stunned the seated man's face got a peculiar look and went ashen. A faint whisper of 'Marlon (MARLIN) Brando' returned his color but he was obviously shaken. Scooting forward he confided his closest friend, coincidently named Wally Cox, recently drowned while fishing. Wow...

A sweetie accompanied by an obviously older domineering husband exhibited little to no self-esteem. Body language alone betrayed her. The thought was perhaps extracting a good memory would put some pep into her step. Very directly, she was told it felt as though I was meant to remind her of a childhood accomplishment. Probably something very minuscule that only she would think was a really big deal. Perplexed she tucked her hair back in a denying headshake flashing an outdated pair of dangly peacock feather earrings. Charmed I unexpectedly went on about a neat trick of balancing the colorful bird plumes, learned from a juggler named Sir Drops-A-Lot. Her shoulders straightened in an upward pride. "Oh, my god I do remember! As a kid, my parents took us skiing. The Bunny Hill was just too difficult and a slope patrol insisted the group of primary school misfits be moved to level ground for safety. It was so embarrassing but an instructor managed to make it fun with snowy games and a mock Olympic awards ceremony. Wow, it actually turned out as one of the best days of my life. Beating out everyone else I balanced a pole on my palm the longest. I even got a blue ribbon for that!"

Wrapping up a smooth reading, ripples of silky purple and black lace lodged between my ears. This totally wiped out the finishing one word whammy. To conclude the subject was informed there are private doors that should not be opened publicly and we'd reach that impasse. Unsatisfied he asked, "What does that mean?" Explained was the uneasy feeling of entering sleeping chambers where I didn't belong, all the while softly patting him as if to extinguish his curiosity. "Come on tell me, please?" he had caught me in a split-second blushing hesitation so I told him about the posh fabrics. His reply was ecstatic. "Lady I knew you were good but that was fantastic! You're describing my girlfriend's satin teddy; I picked up from the drycleaners yesterday and hung it on the back of my bedroom door!"

The theater of our mind is clever and selectively crafty. Conveniently filtering which data to give significance to and retain. Typically gauged by what we want to hear, wishful thinking or the painful harshness of gullibility. (A more accommodating thought would be vulnerability.) All of these participants were convinced without a doubt that Madame Genu possessed wondrous gifts of insight. Others believed she eavesdropped on thoughts, exhibited frightening psychic powers, or had hooked up with their friends for a 'punking'. Despite Svengali and Twilight Zone references, gasp, moans of denial, giggles, goose bumps, tingly neck or arm hairs don't dare withdraw your hand from their knee-they'll grab you (heaven forbid), anxiously replace it and beg for more!

THE GLUE

The human race as complicated and diverse of a genus is more alike than not. Think of how no two snowflakes are ever exactly the same. While their designs are unique, the fact remains they all come from clouds, consist of water, constitute in cold and melt in warmth. Bypassing the surface differences it is mankind's core needs that make us equals. There are six of these recognized universal wants, our behavior is instinct driven to satisfy one or more of them. The first four, love or contact, significance, security, and variety are vital to survival. The last two, growth and contribution are crucial to fulfillment. Compounding matters our cycles of life have built in obstacles and adjustments with each stage. There must be a consistent balance among them all to be whole and content.

It is your mission as a reader to zoom in on these fundamental traits. By utilizing psychological principles that pertain to nearly everyone, you have an opportunity to discern distinguishing qualities.

Employed here is the Forer Effect (Barnum Effect):

You have a need for other people to admire or like you, and yet you tend to be critical of yourself.

While you have some personality weaknesses, you are generally able to compensate for them.

You have considerable unused capacity that you have not turned to your advantage.

Your sexual adjustment or orientation has presented some problems for you.

At times, you have serious doubts as to whether you have made the appropriate decision or done the right thing.

You prefer a certain amount of change in addition to variety and become dissatisfied when hemmed in by restrictions or limitations.

You also pride yourself as an independent thinker; and do not accept other's statements without satisfactory proof.

However, you have found it unwise to be too frank in revealing yourself to others.

At times, you are extroverted, affable, and sociable, while at other times you are introverted, wary and reserved.

Some of your aspirations tend to be rather unrealistic.

Mr. Forer, a psychologist, gave his students personality questionnaires, disregarded their answers, and provided them each with the above blanket final analysis. They were then asked to evaluate the veracity of these results. Since the 1940's this method has been continually published and repeated sustaining a success rate of 84%. When there is benefit of physical and visual interaction the percentage automatically sky rockets! You, you, and yes again, you-sound familiar? FYI: The forward is a homespun example.

In other words, these statements (our stabilizing glue) and the following knee indicators can each stand on their own. Coupling both techniques provides a vast mix of options. However that is just the mechanics what brings depth or texture is your spin, flexibility and finesse. You read between the lines and they will fill in the blanks.

Interpreting the Knee

Looking gorgeous, feeling jazzed, pheromones are flying, the new knee is waiting and you are about to take that quantum leap of faith to orchestrate a happiness scavenger hunt. Whoosh! Anticipation will be half the fun especially since neither of you is capable of forecasting what wonders shall unfold. Relax, charging a room with electromagnetic pizzazz is not an accident. You're in accord with universal canons here so expect great things and the cosmos will deliver. Tallyho!

Instruct a subject to uncover their left knee as it's in line with the heart and has stronger vibrations. Okay, there is one itty-bitty liberty Madame Genu occasionally took with recognizable blowhards for the sake of her own amusement. Continue clarifying terms of a Reading but gently pat or rub the right thigh. Subconsciously this incites them to expose the wrong knee. Gallantly offer to help roll up the correct pant leg; thrown off kilter they are right where you want. Mentioning 'free knee massage' tranquilizes shy or nervous sorts make sure to assist them anyway.

POSITION I
Once a knee is fully revealed, get it in the extended position. This is a temporary angle to gauge the participant's mood and state of well being. Arrange their lower leg across your knees or lap supporting the ankle-avoiding garment interference. While adjusting apply light thumb pressure (no vice grip) in a meaty portion above the patella, upon release note how long it takes area to regain color. If it remains white after a several seconds, they're retaining excess fluids which affect the entire circulatory system. It is really for your calculations but if questioned go ahead and relay the results. A knee caps' mobility resides in synovial fluid; the

'Sea of Sensitivity' for our purposes. Its' condition reflects a person's current attitude towards you and/or the Knee Reading experience.

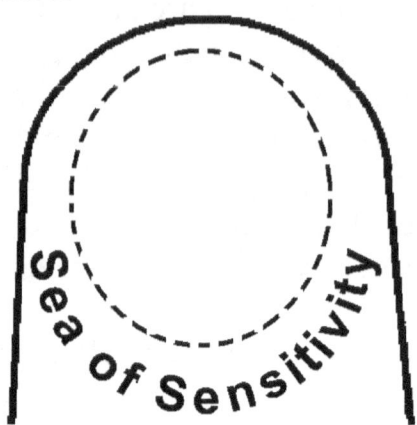

With the utmost care, secure the kneecap itself between your fingertips as in testing the waters so to speak or degrees of mobility.

1st manipulation: the patella slides easily. The patron is open, comfortable and cooperative.

2nd manipulation: kneecap shows some resistance but will move with a little effort. Subject has some reservations and may be unsure of the situation or themselves.

3rd manipulation: the patella is extremely difficult to loosen. This is someone equally stubborn to emotionally budge. They are stressed, fearful or hostile. Announce the client isn't inclined to take the proceedings seriously yet one can tell he is a good sport! Seeding the thought to play along it might be a kick!

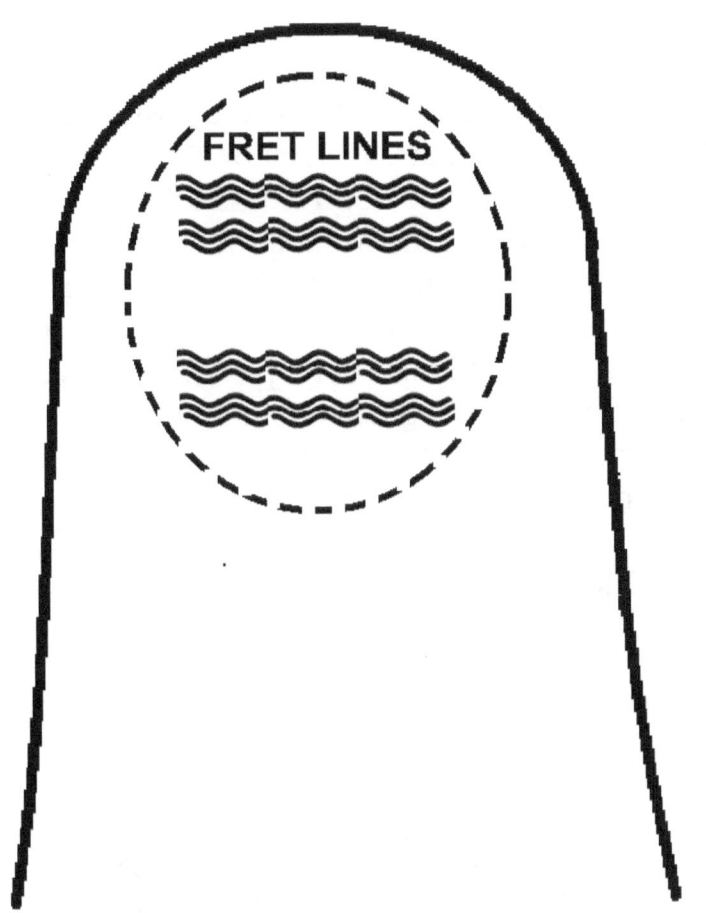

Probe for fret wrinkles, the squiggly lines running horizontally across the mid and/or lower portions of a kneepan. Seen from the median up they are usually job, future stability or control related issues. This person may be inclined to suffer headaches, sinus infections, neck pain and earaches. If located on the bottom half, concerns have a tendency to be about family and safety. One is likely to endure stomach ailments, gas, rashes and restless sleep. When both are present, you've got a worrywart. They are prone to insomnia, heartburn, acid reflex, ulcers, blotches, acne, chewed nails and hair loss. Deriving anxiety origins as work, home or wherever else is fine but keep the laundry list of illnesses to one's self.

POSITION II

The second phase involves the flexed position.
Lower their limb onto your chair run or shoeshine box.
You can straddle their knee or go sidesaddle.
Settled, cup your hand partly around the knee's curvature.
Then trace a cross on the patella surface with your thumb.
Inexplicitly this is where any giggles subside and suddenly
you're no longer a fruit loop. Perhaps it's a well-versed tone
or the realization mystical gears are in motion.
Patter: the knee is divided into four quadrants.
Run the thumb around the exterior pointing them out.

Patter: the 1ˢᵗ section regards intellect
       2ⁿᵈ section will anent fortes
       3ʳᵈ section refers to instincts & the
       4ᵗʰ section is sensitivities (drawn out Elvis style).

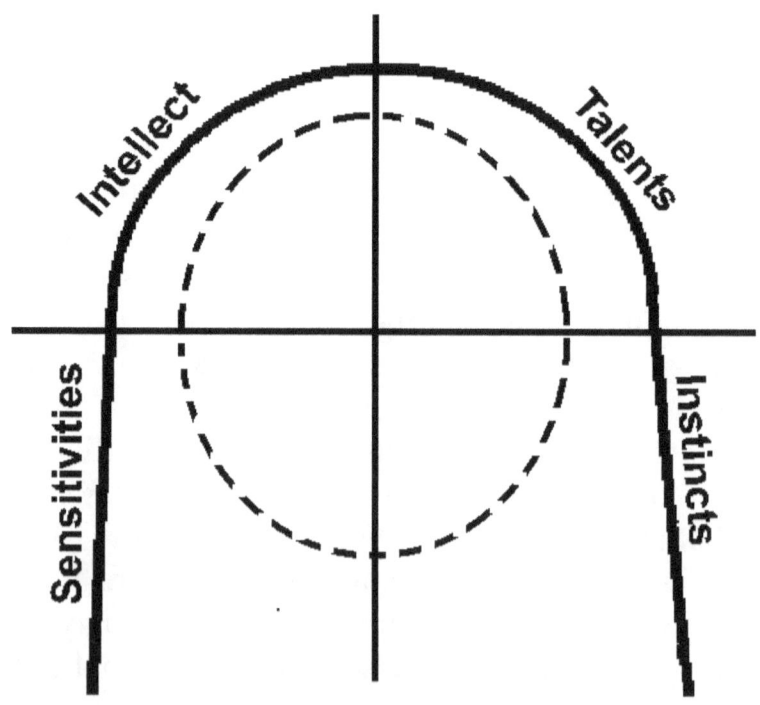

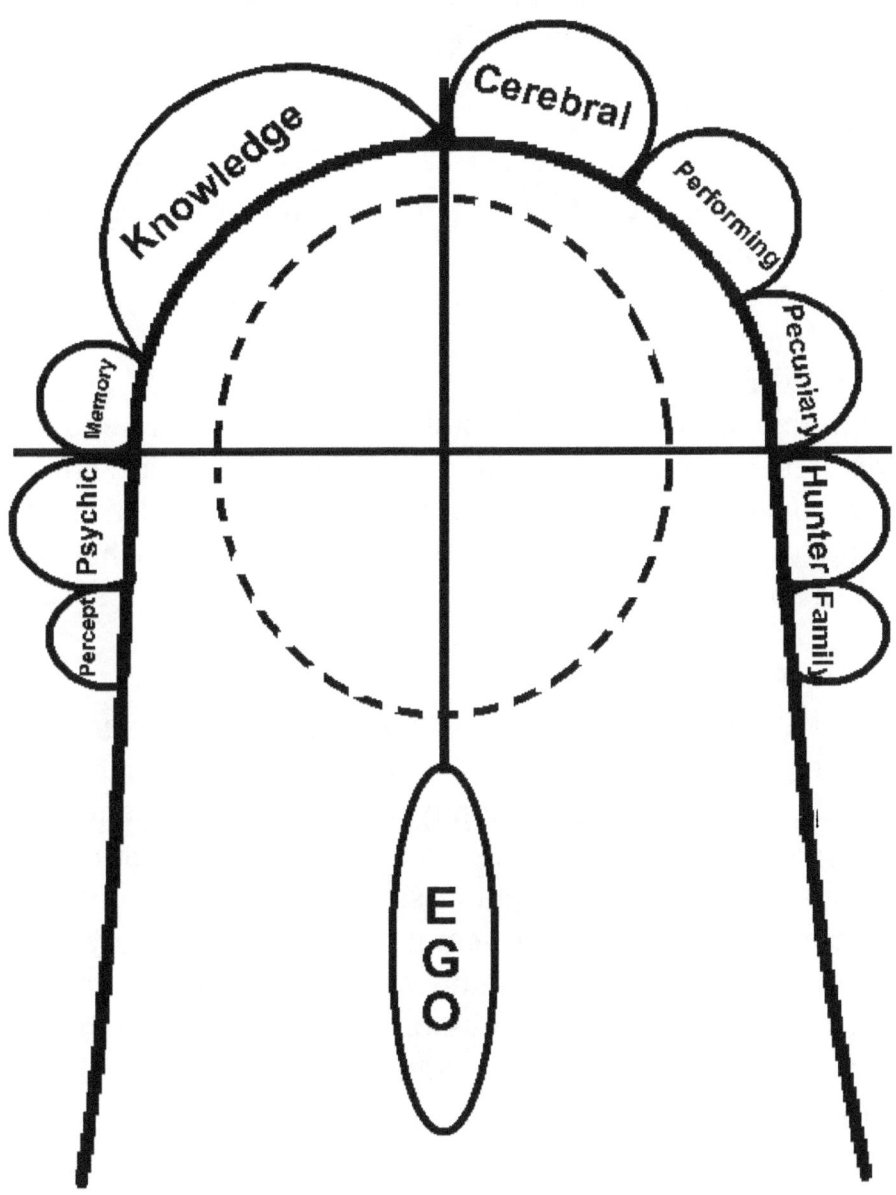

Each region's geography depicts associated features.
Gypsy's vast terrain consisted of over 30 mass or crater
identifiers. Simplified our focus is on the lumps and knobs.
(Plus we have the 'Glue'.) Cultivate the unique synergy
from both techniques and sustain physical contact.

As Captain commence in grandeur, romance affirmations, take baby steps and set the pace to suit yourself. Commandeer a voyage anchoring at the seat of thought following a format of addressing significant factors as you go. Advance with placid kindness, wisdom and your moral compass in tow. Synchronicity at its' best!

KNOWLEDGE KNOLL

This is the only trait all knees possess. Size corresponds directly with a level of intelligence, meaning the bigger the brainier. Should you happen across an exceptionally large one slanting towards the left it is a sign of possible genius.

MEMORY CUSP

When this hill is present, it implies strength to learn and even a better ability for recall. A recollection wizard and asset concerning: phone numbers, addresses, anniversaries, birthdays, crossword puzzles, two buck bets, game shows and trivia.

CEREBRAL ARTS PEAK

Chances are you are dealing with an interesting dexterous mind preoccupied but professionally dedicated-astute in science, engineering, philosophy, technology, mathematics or medicine. Sometimes this is an odd duck indifferent to emotional and physical ineptness: occasionally perceived as intensely arrogant, uptight, remote or distracted. They're just busy trying to figure out how things work in the grand scheme. Sort of a nutty professor- capable of seeing the world in a 360 degree swoop with complete clarity, yet oblivious to what is in front of their face.

PERFORMING ARTS PEAK
Considered as the most common and versatile marker among knees. The patron is inclined to be that people person with a flair for theatrics suggesting 'the life of the party' or a performer. They are typically creative, entertaining and charismatic with or without the gift of gab. Remember though 'All the world's a stage', that makes for a lot of different disguises.

PECUNIARY ARTS PEAK
The knack here is a propensity for acquiring money, someone who is likely to be skilled in business, high finances, gambling or gold digging (both kinds). Keep in mind the 'Midas' touch doesn't guarantee a big spender or exclude penny pinching and economic recklessness.

HUNTER'S HILL
Maybe you've discovered an overgrown Boy or Girl Scout. Many of the same honorable attributes apply: trustworthy, loyal, civilly obedient, dutiful, kind, clean, courteous, friendly, strong, brave and protective. Openly enjoying the camaraderie of healthy competition they can display a zest for life, thriving on and appreciating all the rich amenities nature has to offer.

FAMILY TREE CERES PEAK
This mound mimics a 'stick-in-the-mud', one who is reluctant to venture too far away from deep family attachments or obligations. Frequently a homebody blissfully counting their blessings however that fuddy-duddy could actually be the neighborhood's rescuing bright white light.

PERCEPTION PINNACLE

You have located an observant understanding soul, the consistently empathetic friend or source of great comfort. They are usually generous and accommodating to a fault, forgoing consideration for their own needs. Yes, too often the holders of hands and wipers of tears.

PSYCHIC SUMMIT

This may be a fateful find, 'preaching to the choir' or meeting your match. They are insightful in their own right whatever that may entail parenting, counseling, teaching, tarot, channeling or even palmistry. Utilize their gifts you might learn something about yourself which can bring out your finest.

When you plan to end a reading do it at the Ego Bump. Conclude by gingerly stroking from a kneecaps' bottom edge to approximately 4" down the tibia's ridge. Instead of a cluttered analysis, grab the first word that comes to mind. Enough evidence has already transpired for a fair conclusion plus its' topical appearance speaks for itself. Blurt or milk the tidy observation, your choice. Guide their hand there encouraging the subject to validate it for himself. Go ahead invite other interested parties to cop a feel!

The finishing touch is last but certainly not least. Those felicitous stamp impressions stick around awhile. Folks will depart satisfied having an inky token of proof and something interesting to share about themselves. Wa La!

Congratulations well done, encore!

Knee Knowledge

Knowledge is power,
Power evokes strength
& Knees are strong.

Exposing just a 'tip of the tibia' is this brave attempt to articulate knee wisdoms Madame Genu acquired on her wondrous travels. The realm of knees reaches far into our core existence spanning throughout history and the world. It's a vast spectrum deeply influenced by the crisscrossing of cultural and geographic values. Imprints are embedded all along the corridors of life. Their mysterious paths offer an array of avenues from sacred territories to the back yard.

Exploring these horizons enlightens the view. Enjoy a remarkable journey getting reacquainted with your subject. Embrace the opportunity to establish a resourceful foundation. You'll be rewarded with precious tokens while gaining strength and self-assurance. (Note with so many knees and so little time there are frontiers still to be ventured; art, construction, dance, literature, medicine, music, religion, nature, science, sports, and technology.)

Knee knowledge should be of endearment and shared with the same tenderness in which it is discovered. There's no need or pleasure in forced informative arrogance. Let it transcend as an accompaniment to experiences. A fruitful trail waits, you will happily find 'to know knee is to love knee'.

ANATOMY

The knee joint is an extraordinary component of the human anatomy with a multitude of duties. Knees carry the load of our form, support stability, act as shock absorbers, and provide capability for motion. Humbly they withstand constant use and stress. Including but not limited to crawling, kneeling, standing, walking, running, hopping, skipping, jumping and kicking. In certain activities, the knee is subject to nearly ten times the body's weight. With such important responsibilities, it's hard to imagine how easily we dismiss and ignore the knee.

As the largest joint of our structure, it is the connection point of the upper and lower leg. This union is made with three bones, two major ligament groups, and cartilage all enclosed in a fibrous sack.

First, the heaviest, strongest and longest bone of our frame-the femur. Often called the thighbone it actually makes up almost a quarter of our total height. The bottom end has two knuckle-like ball shaped projections called condyles. Top of the sturdy tibia or shinbone also has two condyles. These are simpler and flatter with a rounded bowl type indent. This design makes for a perfect match and fit with the femoral condyles. Between the bones are two crescent pads called menisci, which is the ruff elastic connective tissue (cartilage) that prevents them from scraping together. Attached on the tibia side these cushions disperse compressions and enable the femur to easily glide into different positions:

FLEXION-BENDING OF KNEE
EXTENSION-STRAIGHTENING OF KNEE
ROTATION-TURNING OF KNEE (LIMITED)

Shielding this function is the patella (kneecap). 2-3 inches wide and 3-4 inches tall, similar to an upside down tear drop. Embedded in a tendon it follows in conjunction with femur movements, assisting leverage while serving as a durable protective cover.

Joining knee bones are ligaments, stretchy bands of strong tissue. Cruciates criss-cross beneath the kneecap, a collateral pair runs along outside edges. Some folks reveal daring feats of patella relocation, claiming double-jointed knees. No such thing, their ligaments are merely hyper-mobile.

Keeping everything intact, is a mesh Synovial Capsule encasing and bonding the knee joint mechanics. Ensuring a

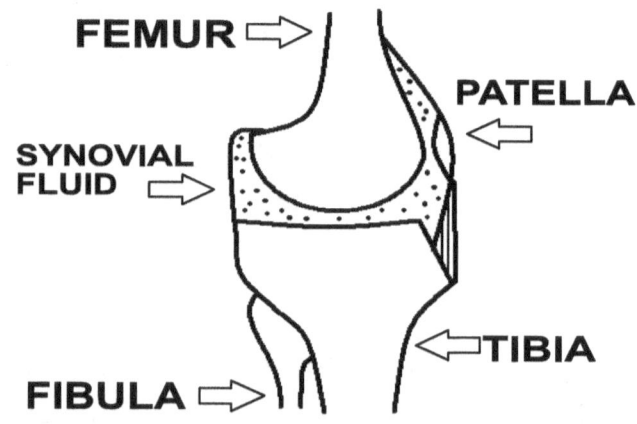

(KNEE JOINT IN EXTENSION-STRAIGHT)

smooth operational relationship it is lined with a fine membrane secreting small amounts of a fortifying thick synovial lubricant. The knee's very own self-contained lube and oil shop.

Every year millions of people of all ages seek medical attention for knee problems. There are several contributing factors such as degeneration (due to aging or disease), injuries and diet. For every pound one loses, it takes off 4 pounds of pressure across the knees, proving weight is a serious issue too.

When fluids become unhealthy or irritated they accumulate and leak in or around the workings becoming painfully inflamed. Case in point housemaid's knees, a name

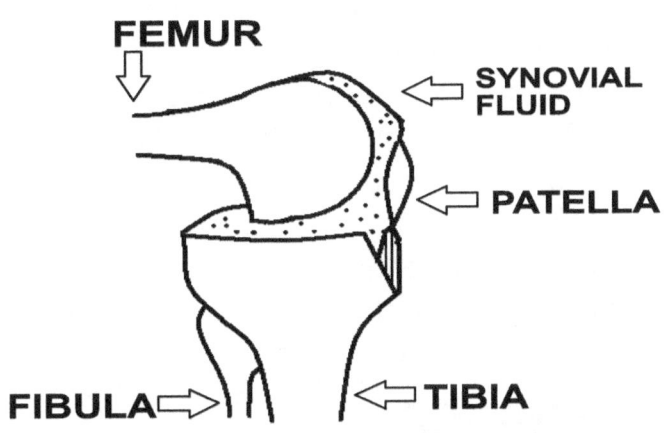

(KNEE JOINT IN FLEXION-BENT)

assigned to a very agitated state usually associated with occupations involving long periods of kneeling. As levels increase this 'water on the knee' can only be relieved by draining. Hot swollen joints can be rheumatoid arthritis, gout or infection. Cold hard joints covered in tight shinny skin are more apt to be signs of osteoarthritis. Left untreated these conditions can lead to crippling disabilities.

Jealous Knee Syndrome (JKS) is a disorder resulting from surgery and stir craziness. Symptoms are neurotic episodes where one knee misbehaves in retaliation to the other's constant attention. Obviously, it's annoying.

Behind the knee is very sensitive and useful with thin soft skin. Toxins are expelled here and perfume is enhanced on the pulse point. It is targeted as a dangerous tickle spot, credited as a favored erogenous zone.

In 1998 Science magazine reported a prestigious study demonstrating sleep-wake cycles could be adjusted through skin light absorption. Treatments to the back of knees carry 'photic' indicators up to the brain resetting signals. This is one of those discoveries that is challenged and reconsidered every few years.

Italians have findings knee arthritis is the first warning of lung cancer. Often such tumors removed subsides knee pain.

Knees play an intricate multi taxing role in the body's circulatory system. Wearing shorts really does help to cool down. Holding a cold can of soda pop tucked up under the knee crease rapidly changes your core temperature. Standing perfectly erect for a long time with knees locked (especially in the heat) restricts blood flow making one susceptible to fainting. Unconsciousness may be avoided by sitting with your head between your knees. According to Dutch researchers, crossing legs may also prevent fainting. According to mom, crossing legs or keeping your knees touching is the proper and ladylike way to sit. Later she will be telling you that crossing legs potentially causes varicose veins.

Girls raised on cod liver oil have legs like this !!

Girls who ride horses have legs like this ( )

Girls who sit at bars have legs like this) (

But... little girls who were well brought up cross their legs like this X

When seated the space from your waist to knees is a lap. An instant portable spare seat or table plus pull up your knees to rest hands and head-what a deal! Recognizing the unlimited contributions of the knee can greatly enrich your confidence and readings.

THE BABY IN KNEE

Babies' knees have an irresistible quality as one of the sweetest and most innocent things on earth, thus deserving to be addressed independently. Chubby, dimpled and oh so ticklish baby knees are cute. Baring those in public is always welcome. Moms openly adore them no matter how old you are, squeezed to oochee-goochee and tenderly pinched for luck.

Trivia flourishes in current culture feeding the belief babies are born without kneecaps and they are not fully established until two years of age. I prefer this interpretation it sounds quaint and less painful for expectant mothers. To be fair it's a matter of perception, Gray's Anatomy states a cartilage tissue formed late in fetal growth is a seedling for the patella. Developing into bone it must first ossify, occurring at about 3 years for girls and 4-5 years for boys. Depending on when you think, a kneecap is actually a knee-cap, before or after ossification determines your opinion.

Typically, at 6-8 month's babies start rocking or pushing off from their knees initiating crawling. This first mode of locomotion strengthens the legs so as to be able to walk and stand. Once tykes reach the stage of standing unaided at mother's knee they are referred to as knee biters, knee huggers, and toddlers. Barin is a centuries old common Scottish term for baby. Gluin barin (knee baby) is a young one tittered on your knee before they learn to walk. Knee baby American style is southern regional slang for the second youngest child. This may have been to distinguish them from the baby and/or that they had grown knee high.

The knee-to-chest burp (flexing the little one's knees up against their chest) helps pass excess gas in both directions! Fussy babies are instinctively calmed and entertained by knee bouncing. Bobbing a youngster up and down on your knee-modern research has shown combining this rhythm with song wires the brain's sensory system. Dandling is an outdated word for playfully bumping and dancing a small fry on your knee. The childish chants and teaching songs exist with all nationalities and begin the life lessons learned at mother's knee. Join in a brisk po-knee ride down memory lane:

> Head and shoulders, knees and toes,
> Knees and toes, knees and toes.
> Head and shoulders, knees and toes,
> Knees and toes, knees and toes.

> Toe knee chest nut nose eye love you
> Toe knee chest nut nose eye love you.
> Toe knee chest nut nose eye love you.
> That's what toe knee chest nut nose.

> *Hands on shoulders*
> *Hands on knees*
> *Hands behind you*
> *If you please!*

> The ants go marching 3 by 3, hooray, hooray
> The ants go marching 3 by 3, hooray, hooray
> The ants go marching 3 by 3,
> The little one stopped to scratch his knee

> Oh, Susanna,
> Oh, don't you cry for me,
> I come from Alabama,
> With my banjo on my knee.

> YOUR LEG BONE CONNECTED TO YOUR KNEE BONE,
> YOUR KNEE BONE CONNECTED TO YOUR THIGH BONE.

One, two, three,
Baby's on my knee
One, two, three, four,
Oops! Baby's on the floor!

This old man, he played three,
He played knick knack on my knee,
With a
Knick, knack, paddy whack,
Give the dog a bone;
This old man came rolling home.

I went to the Animal Fair
The birds and the beast were there
The big baboon by the light of the moon
Was combing his auburn hair

The monkey got drunk,
And fell on the elephant's trunk,
The elephant sneezed and fell on his knees,
And that was the end of the monkey, monkey, monkey...

Three sailors went to knee, knee, knee
To see what they could knee, knee, knee
But all they could knee, knee, knee
Was the bottom of the deep blue knee, knee, knee
Three sailors went to knee, knee, knee
To see what they could knee, knee, knee
But all they could knee, knee, knee
Was the bottom of the deep blue knee, knee, knee!

Shocking, shocking, shocking,
A mouse ran up my stocking.
What did it see when it got to the knee?
Oh, shocking, shocking, shocking!

Bumble Bee, Bumble Bee
By the Tree,
Bumble Bee gets Johnny,
Under the Knee.

ON MY HEAD THERE IS A FLEA
NOW HE'S CLIMBING DOWN ON ME
PAST MY BELLY, PAST MY KNEE
ON MY TOE...OH LET ME BE!

'It takes a village to raise a child' could have stemmed from various worldwide examples of passing the baby knee to knee. Several gatherings welcoming off spring into the community, naming them or even adoption are knee related. An old Northern Ireland version involves the bean ghluin (midwife) known as 'woman of the generation'. Bean translates to woman and since gluin is Irish for generation or knee, the language permits for an implication of passing a child knee to knee.

Another early birthing ritual 'treating of the knee' is Georgian. A sweet corn or wheat flour mush is offered to the woman in childbed, her midwife and to all females present. The next day this porridge is handed from knee to knee sharing it with family and guest in a celebratory gesture. Likewise, Mayan Indians had a blessing of life meal for the midwife and attendants. Among Navajo people, whoever makes a baby laugh first is privileged to host the greeting feast. This station is honored by having said wee-one held on their lap during the joyous festivities. (Yep, that convenient tuck is always the best seat in the house!)

Laps are a very accommodating design for infants their heads nestle naturally between the knees providing closeness and security. A cozy haven, it would be nice to think 'lap of luxury' originated for them. Laying a babe face down across the knees while gently rubbing or patting their back is good for burping and very soothing. As they age the same position is used for spanking. Unfortunately, sitting on Santa's knee or lap has been banned in England shopping centers (citing child endangerment) and is now spreading to U.S. malls.

There are plenty of colorful childbearing concepts. Wearing straw knee garters ensures fertility. Seashell ones increase the odds a female will procreate children. Wheat straw knee bands encourages having a boy. Oak straw knee wreaths promote little girls. Several deep knee bends induces labor. Kneeling and squatting methods in delivery. Constantly crossing one's legs means the darling babe will probably be birthed with knees crossed. If your bambino arrives fat his wrinkles from bended knee to upper thigh foretells the number of future births. Yikes!

The maternal kinship is inherent with baby knees as is babies on knees. Revolving throughout time, they have been tools for nurturing, bonding and forging the life force spirit.

SAVE KNEE, SAVE KNEE!

A waterfront weekend engagement uncovered a notion so clever it was almost cunning. Neatly rolling up a pant leg was a pleasant yet rather nondescript fellow. Unexpectedly he showed a very fine knee! Gushing about how he should be one of those hunky UPS guys was over the top but unavoidable. The quicksilver blush couldn't be denied as he slowly shook his head in disbelief. Instead of retreating, he calmly replied his delivery days were over long ago.

It didn't matter what I said after that, a UPS connection had already set the reading for success. The bonus here was a smart technique used to test drivers. He told of a unique way a marble was utilized to ensure knees would be properly bent while lifting to avoid back problems. Keeping a round bobble from rolling out of the front breast pocket is not that easy if you are transferring packages up and down. Routine checks were made monitoring its' condition, the marks and scratches were rated as failed attempts of proper lifting. The idea was justified with the company because it limited medical injury claims. Though grading in this manner gave no merit to driving abilities so the union got the procedure terminated. Still the story was just too good to be true he had to be teasing.

The next evening the bartender joyously waved a small bulging manila coin envelope, left by a patron for me. Popping it open, a brown opaque glass sphere slipped into my hand. Upon closer inspection, scrapes and scars marred an incandescent sheen. This was evidence from the fore mentioned courier's personal experience, what a guy! Validated and verified the information turned out to be factually based. What an ingenious knee defense for sparing one from strain. Kudos!

To drop a male attacker, knee him in the crotch. Because this is a universal move and anticipated, it may not be so effective. For escape purposes only (causes extreme damage) bring knee up and swiftly drive the foot out, stomping their knee with your heel. This can be done from the front, side, or even the back. If snatched from behind fall on your knees (not to beg) to put them off balance. Try to grab around their knees not letting go making it difficult to relocate you. Even a bop in the chin with your knee is a painful deterrent.

Urban legend claims an aspirin, nickel or quarter clamped tightly between the knees during sexual relations is a sure-fire birth control method. WARNING! FICTION!

In the 1950's schools had standard 'Atomic Bomb' drills. Teachers would lead classes to basements, under tables, and away from windows. To be safe children would be instructed to crouch, cover ears and put their head between the knees. Was this really supposed to save you from a nuclear blast?

CIVIL DEFENSE-DUCK AND COVER

In an earthquake drop immediately to the ground and crawl away from objects that may fall on you. Doors can swing violently so it's no longer suggested to brace yourself in the frame. Under a sturdy desk or table put your head between knees then cover with hands.

Tornadoes are frightening, the sky looks strange and static makes your hair stand on end. Never lie down flat instead squat and put head between your knees.

When lightning strikes it's trying to take the path of lease resistance. To keep out of that electric circuit find a low area avoiding trees, poles, and freestanding structures. Point being is to have the least amount of grounding contact by making ones' self the smallest target possible. Start by crouching down close to the ground on the balls of your feet. Then put hands over ears and head between knees.

EMERGENCY LANDING POSITION
HEAD BETWEEN YOUR KNEES!

This is a test. This is only a test. Had this been a real emergency you would have been instructed to put your head between your knees and pray.

If all else fails put your head between your knees and kiss your ass goodbye!

EE-KNEE
ME-KNEE
MY-KNEE
MO

KNEE AID-

Conceivably Neanderthals gathered spare animal skin scraps to cover their knobs from cold temperatures or hunting abrasions and cuts. By putting straw and dried grasses under loose hides, lengthy kneeling was softened. Common sense! Preventive measures fueled necessity and a never-ending procession of knee protection ensued.

1000 BC Mayans engaged in 'ball games' that were intense and extravagant public events. Playing fields were located within the nerve centers of their communities and held sacred as well as social values. The team players' costumes were lavish including an illustrious single ornate kneepad. Remaining artifacts support the participant's grand attire but not rules or end results.

Encountered in 1965-66 Bulgarian excavations of the Vratsa Treasure was an exquisite warrior's knee piece. Embossed with elaborate artwork, perfectly symmetrical and dating back to early 4th century BC.

Egyptian Coptic techniques adorned garments in the late third century BC. Specifically orbiculums, oval or square tapestry patches placed at the kneepan area so as to minimize joint damage. More than likely a cousin of Gypsy's Khet patch.

Armor sheltered patellae during the 13th to 15th centuries, which was better suited for battles. A combination of defense devices were assembled; knee cops, cups, rondels, chain mail, plate, gutters, quilted greaves, and poleyns. As aegis developed up to three lames (heart shaped wings) were added to accommodate for the backside and articulation.

The Knee Defender is a retail product currently on the market for shielding knees of long legged passengers on airplane flights. Many religions have prayer mats, cushions, throws or fold down pew kneelers fulfilling traditions and comfort. A variety of kneepads such as molded plastic, spongy or non-skid rubber are proven essential equipment for construction crews and gardeners. Statistically it's sports that provide the largest arena requiring padded gear to safeguard knees.

FYI: The distance between your knee and ankle is the same from your elbow to fingertips (adult).

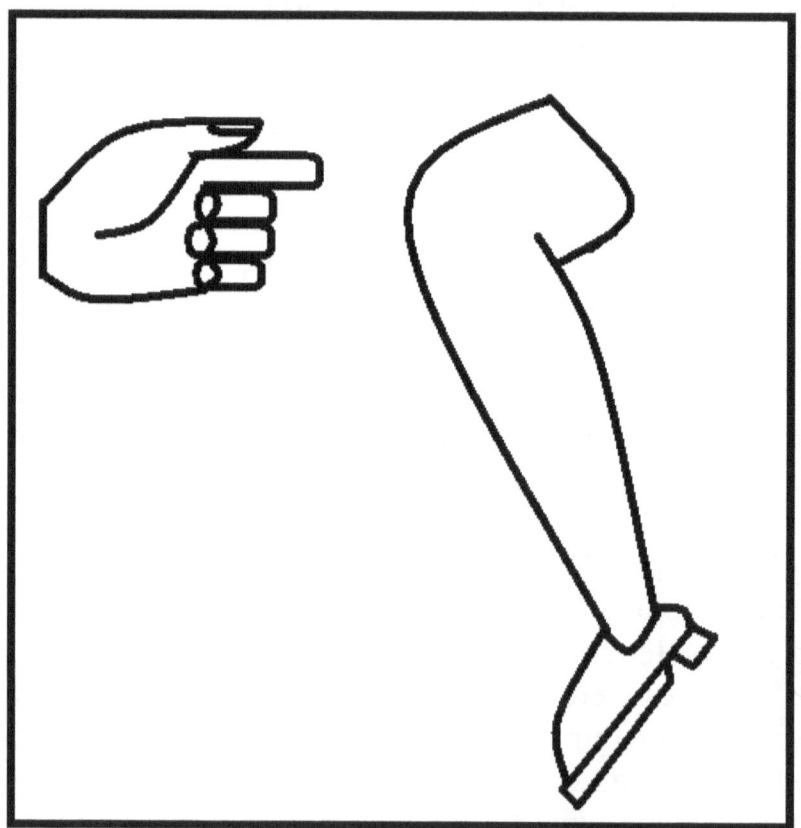

When you have accidentally bumped your knee:

#1-make a wish by saying, 'Bee's knee, Knee be.' or
#2-hold a hand on both knees to make a wish.

KNEE FASHION

Our fashion sense satisfies needs and desires stimulated by; celebration of religious or social events, showing association affiliations , identifying one's status within a group, sexual attraction, and expressing individuality. These basics continue to prosper while being environmentally and economically sensitive. The way we dress mirrors these personal attitudes-good, bad or indifferent.

In some wrinkle along global clotheslines, knees were drafted as a meter, the body's reference point of stockings, boots and hems. Typically items are gauged so many inches above, below or at the knee. Perhaps it started with working class Egyptians wearing knee length togas whereas those of higher stature had longer tunics. Who's to say? Sorting through the world's wardrobe closet is too overwhelming and why this writer has chosen not to enter until the 20th century.

In the early 1900's an Edwardian air of excessive and flamboyant ground sweeping dresses prevailed. Boys and young men would don tight fitting 'doubled kneed' breeches that met high knee stockings, knickerbockers (banded beneath the knee) or short britches. Graduating towards long trousers had become a right of passage into manhood. With motoring the hobble skirt emerged it was respectfully shorter, a yard around with a knee high side slit to allow for walking and stepping up to trains, trolleys or Model Ts.

By 1910, daring swimming costumes surfaced with the accessibility of seaside beaches and spas. Men's togs were one or two-pieces resembling long johns, concealing chest hair and their knees. Women's bathers modestly hid everything, below the knee bloomers over woven socks or leggings. These swimsuits could weigh up to 20 lbs. when wet. Dapper gents wore golf apparel consisting of 4 plus knickers with matching argyles, vest and cap. There were 4 plus, 6 plus, 8 plus and 10 plus varieties. 'Plus' relates to how many inches below the knee they hung. Boy Scouts of America had built up their momentum prompting hiking and camping situpons. An ending of overseas military action motivated a patriotic verve to their official uniforms, short pants and turn over top knee high socks.

Great Grandma Billie was 19 in 1926; she could have been a poster girl for the infamous 'Roaring Twenties'. It was the hay day for flappers a saucy radical breed of modern young females that blossomed after WW1. They were rebelling against their feminist mothers and grandmothers who had become tired or prudish. A brazen lot sporting boyish bobs, face powder, lipstick, rouge and dark circling around the eyes. Makeup had previously been reserved for actresses and harlots. Scandalous! Recklessly they road community transportation (motorcycles in Billie's case-so shocking), boldly smoked, were defiant to prohibition, and shamelessly attended petting parties. Discarding corsets, sleek Jazz inspired attire was adopted. Waistlines dropped to the hips and skirts rose to their knees. Grandma had said rayon stockings were rolled, twisted or gartered. Rouging of knees was just in the movies-be serious girl stains! The trick was to get them just a whisper above a hem. This allowed for flashing racy glimpses of their knees while walking in a breeze or better yet flaunting them in the latest dance craze. They thrived on decadent high kicks, enticing knee swirls, and illusionary criss-crossing of the Charleston. It was all the rage and gave knees center stage, as well should be.

1930's brought the Great Depression. A frugal and sparse mood couldn't uphold such a spirited life style.

Hems dropped several inches and the spotlight veered from knees and frivolous antics. Less cumbersome accouterments became more acceptable in a practical overhauled form. Skirts had below knee paneled pleats to add dimension; they were longer in the back than front. College fellows slipped long pants 'Oxford Bags' measured from 22" to 40" around the bottoms over their now academically forbidden knickers. Serving as a distraction to their struggles cinema's chic glamour captured public imagination while dictating the direction of what was vogue.

1940's propaganda with advertising instilled a wartime mentality of 'use it up, wear it out, and make it do or do without'. There was rationing of coveted ladies stockings (hubba-hubba) and yardage but not garters. Out of resourcefulness, pillowcases were reassembled into white shorts for summer. Sensible all seasonal, utility, tailored and outdoor clothing simplified silhouettes.

1950's America was regaining its' financial equilibrium and a crisp feeling of hopeful opportunity excelled. Moms stylishly entertained; barbeques in tapered slacks tied with shoestring laces at the knees, over knee stretch pants and tight pedal pushers. Bandstand and knee dusters were keen, extremely full circle skirts with scratchy netting or starched petticoats underneath (as many as possible). Guys were comfortable baring their knees in Bermudas while girls could really show off their legs in short shorts.

Swabbies are navy issued work denim dungarees, so called for their ability to easily be folded up keeping them dry while swabbing the deck. Belled at the knees they were also used as a lifesaving floatation device. A civic activated youth of the 1960's made a major political and trend statement when they got bellbottoms from military surplus outlets or thrift shops. Acknowledged as hippies the flower children 'addicted to love' and opposed to Vietnam. Bells were a unisex pant decorated in embroidery, studs, rhinestones, assorted symbols, appliqués, calico hand sewn knee patches and beads. To be really groovy these or any jeans had outer leg seams split up to the knee filled in with a triangle of fabric. Some were so wide they were nicknamed 'elephant bells'. Starting out conservative straight skirts had front and back inverted flaps called kick pleats allowing knees to move freely to do the twist. Parochial schools shared similar skirt length dress codes with public institutions. They also had a common with the girls rolling waistbands to hitch up their skirts. Violators were sent to the principle/headmaster to be measured, no more than 2 inches above their knees or sent home! By the time one made it to his/her office a little adjustment and presto problem solved! Then England went mod exposing us to 'mini' skirts resting 6-8 inches above the knee, mercy! Very short cheeky 'sizzle dresses', same patterned panties and thigh high boots soon followed.

The 1970's scene contemplated self-awareness nurturing farout looks. Gaucho Pants, patella covering robust Mexican flavored culottes accented with knee high laced up suede boots. 'Hot Pants' which were even higher above the knee than micro mini skirts while providing a wink of mystery. Disco fever hit big, couples boogied down in loose dreamy knee length dresses and flared (smaller bells) synthetic trousers or jump suits. Loud trippy psychedelic prints and polyester was everywhere! Later seen glittered knee-highs (striped or solid) and Baby Boos hot pink socks that went from the knee to ankle. Status driven designer labels saturated the market giving peer pressure a whole new voice. Sears introduced a unique 'tri-blend' pant for ruff and tumble children that had reinforced knees. Their company slogan guaranteed your kids would out grow the durable jeans before they wore out. Go -'Toughskins'!

The glossy 1980's yielded several fads. Preppy kilts and knee socks, akin to the coming of age naughty schoolgirl outfit that has always had a provocative allure. Pastel female-buttoned knickers accompanied by nylon knee hi stockings. Daisy Dukes', super short fitted denim cut offs cheered on by a TV program. Color-coordinated, specked, sparkled and fluorescent dancer knee warmers (tubular knits) were a huge commodity over tights, under short skirts, with sweats, bunched or extended. There were short Lycra leggings that came just below the knees.

Guys had awesome options. Rad parachute pants, nylon britches with exterior zippered knee pockets. Khaki cargo shorts or pants with big flapped pockets to the knee. 'Zip off Shants' that allowed a portion of the pant leg to be zippered and removed at knee level to accommodate weather changes. Some gangs started displaying their group colors by tying a bandana around the knee area. Both genders endorsed battery acid burned and shredded jeans, especially at the knee.

Edgy garments peppered the 1990's. Hardcore road warrior steel toed black leather knee high boots plus chromed shins. Code on cool was to have a single tidy hole about an inch wide above the patella of only one jean leg layered atop black tights. A retro shower of hot pants, mini skirts, striking over the knee stockings as bellbottoms or flares faded 'in' and out. 'Toughskins' experienced an improved rebirth. Eventually the industry tried to mimic Generation X's scruffy 'grunge' styles with beat up ripped knee Gucci blue jeans-instantly selling out for $3715.00 each!

After escaping Y2K and facing off 911, the country took on a serious sobering approach. There was nothing subtle about red, white and blue flooding catwalks. Rows of Fleet Week audience members were noticed sitting with their white Navy dixie-cup caps perched uniformly on the left knees. Was that pride or protocol?

As the atmosphere cleared fresh energy sparked a smashing array of shorts; spandex biking thigh huggers, relaxed athletic trunks, velour, terry cloth, narrow wale corduroy, soft calfskin, vertically pleated, skorts, Capri's, cropped, floaters, tugs, mockers (cuffed knee jeans), camouflage/fatigue knickers, and a brief appearance of delicious sherbet orange or lime Bermudas. Up to several inches below the knee were casual men's mainstream baggy pegtops of white or neutrals, some having large midway stitched zippered or Velcro pockets. Meanwhile Hollywood red carpet gurus claimed full figured women should always wear their frocks to cover the knees. They applauded balloon (bubble) high waist skirts bellowing away from the body and gathered at a knee hem. Eyes were also on 'tulips' updated minis and cardigan sweaters down to the leg hinges. The dollar rule (no more than the width of a bill above the knee) still seemed to govern politically correct job or formal garb. There'd been a faint focus on unusual texture combos such as punked out knee netted and crochet leggings, lacey bellbottom inserts, 'badass' rocker denim flares bearing killer eight inch rectangular cordovan knee patches or creative satin trims. Avant-garde bells surfaced thick legged and high belted. Hip-Hop artist kicked it pushing up left pant legs to the knee. Sports, TV, movie, music and other entertainment celebrities have all been seen in a pair of jeans with a conspicuous threadbare spot or rip on one or both knees-obviously a timeworn favorite.

Disney's Pirates of the Caribbean movie made the Jolly Roger friendly. No article was immune to the Skull and Crossbones. Wicked to whimsical they were captured on scarves, kerchiefs, t-shirts, jewelry, belts, corporate Psycho Bunny-Bear ties, hats, pajamas, sheets, towels, lunch boxes and socks. A knee bone smorgasbord available in department stores as well as Victoria's Secret, pet parlors and baby boutiques. Remember this new millennium is still in its' infancy and the best is yet to come. There's a future of man-made materials that's astounding with promises of nanotech, chemical filtering, wound healing, bug repelling, rebound, climate control, light bending, invisibility, micro-weave, organic, solar, sensor, tracking and electronic fibers. Fashion isn't just fashion anymore!

GARTERS

Garters with their worthy siblings sashes, flashes and tassels are bindings wound above or right below the knee to hold up stockings. They can be made of cloth, metal, cords, leather, soft twigs, ribbons, or braided yarns. Fastened by: tying, tucking, hooking, broaching, lacing, elastic, buckles, snaps, and yes, Velcro.

Their background and value exceeds virginal attributes of a bridal garter. Primitive examples indicate practical and spiritual purposes. Prehistoric spun dog hair finger weaving strips were revealed in dry Arizonan caves. A piece of digit looming from 6,000 to 8,000 years ago was preserved in the wet marshes of Florida. There are 3000-year-old north-eastern pottery relics showing impressions of woven textiles that had been pressed into the clay. Dancing women with ostrich eggshell knee bracelets are seen on South African sand paintings, additionally noted elsewhere on cave dwelling walls. Exploration yielded Viking hooked decorative valances. Wicklebanders, German herringbone spiral knee wraps were also found. For assorted pagans they were enchanted and had magical powers: the witch's belt, a devil's badge, sprite cinches, laurel leg wreaths or serpent coils. There's a unique group where "Black Widow" garters are granted after their secretive initiations. A coven's High Priestess was eligible to add a buckle to her garter for every new cluster split off the hive. This represented a degree of rank whose common legacy circulated into medieval times.

Establishment of 'Order of the Garter' in 1344 with all its' honors and status could have encouraged competitive circumstances. Mottos and caprice end bobbles became prominent. There were demi-garters (also called percloses) which were divided and had logos or crest. Cross-braced garters wrapped below knees then crossed behind to be tied on one side of the top and were thought somewhat pretentious. "I'll have your guts for garters" is a saying certainly spurred out of confrontational intimidations with foes. Much later considered a verbal threat of punishment for naughty children.

In the Elizabethan era it was quite fashionable for British blokes to wear fanciful girts with flare and a touch of vanity, influenced heavily by the regal atmosphere. Scotsmen folded knee socks over a flash of ribbon or tartan tassel, wool to worsted and robustly knotted. Morris dancing has existed in areas of England for over 600 years. In a central style, bells are placed below the knees in another method coconuts are strapped on and act as castanets.

Pilgrim lads bunched baggy breeches above the calf and yoked them with a bow. Eventually U.S. mountain men and trappers would draw on richly pigmented bands or fringed sashes as an extra hand for carrying; knives, horns, supply pouches or pelts. They were aids should one of the travelers fall into water or slip by dire straights. The bright material would increase visibility even in shadows so their comrades could rescue them. Meanwhile eastern woodland Native Americans are accredited with refining their finger lanyard into durable art. French Canadian traders learned and duplicated the technique producing what was named 'Assomption' sashes meant to hold up half leggings, which were successfully marketed abroad.

In 1731, a French explorer brought back a promising sap that South and Central American Indians used for water-proofing. Equivalent plant residues emerged out of Africa, Eastern Asia, and India. About the same time the phrase 'Stars and Garters' appeared referring to tokens of victory or distinction, typically these awards were star shaped. Its' continued deployment resulted in an expletive and/or small oath. Oh, my!

In 1844, processing had introduced rubber giving garters a substantial boost. Enter stage left cancan girls entertained gariter (French) gazing. Early 1900 hundreds presented buskers, street vendors, carnival barkers, and one-man-bands clanging cymbals tied or looped betwixt their knees. It wasn't until 1925 they were able to boil proof elastic, which was just in line for flapper risqué contributions projecting 'the clams' garters' (spiffy) into their flashy vocabulary. Soon to follow a female wartime workforce that could afford to purchase garters which they embroidered with their absent sweethearts' initials. By 1940, men relied on suspender sock garters that are presently available but seriously outdated and tiresome.

Crow, Cheyenne, Sioux, and Arapahoe all incorporated knee laced sheep bells in their dancing. Clackers are sets of deer toes sewn onto leather knee straps that make pleasant melodic clapping sounds. 1850's New York tribes had rattles made from several hoofs strung in rows then attached around the knee; this period also documented animal bone girds in Africa. Zulu warlords strung cow tails beneath the knobs to give an illusion of greater girth. The majority of southeastern Indians wore beaded garters, made with twisted buffalo or opossum hairs. Not to forget the Oklahoma's vibrant feather knee bustles. Andamanese 19th century photographs show small strips and stringed shell decorations encircled above the knees. The Great members would occasionally include knee belts of shells affixed to pandanus leaves to make their motions rustle with rattling noises. Thailand's Padaung adult females don brass rings above and below the knees. The Chickasaw Nation display abundant tasseled red garters about their knees. Shell shaker shackles are a ceremonial pride of the women. Once out of tortoise shells today they may be made from small Pet milk cans with stream pebbles added to ensure maintaining rhythm. Pueblos still dress with traditional multi-colored ribands and bells jingling at the knee to elect their elders.

There are some Midwest American high schools where the girls started wearing garters to spice up their proms. The evenings' end is highlighted by allowing their dates to remove them as keepsakes. At more reserved dances, the female's garter is simply exchanged with her escort's bowtie. It's been said, no man can resist a scented garter.

SUPERSTITIONS

Originally, mortals looked to the gods and elements for guidance. Seeking answers to maneuvering a suspicious unknown. By incorporating external forces, instincts, and social acceptance patterned thoughts emerged. They spread across the planet like gossip. Such as a childhood game of 'Broken Telephone Line' where the last whisper is just a fragment of the first.

This gave birth to life's communal groundwork upheld by customs, folklore, legends, myths, and rituals. All of which can be associated with superstitions, the activities habitually performed in an effort to secure desired outcomes. Governed by the power and control of fears they're attached to vulnerabilities. This has a potent impact on belief structures.

Oddly enough, these practices do not have to make any sense leaving ample room for contradictions and ambiguous behavior. Whether taken seriously or seen as disposable amusement, they have comforted and nourished humanity for thousands of years.

'Break a Leg' is a common expression bestowed amongst actors, play writes and producers. In a reverse psychology ward off bad spirits kind of way, it means 'good luck'. Betwixt theories of origin is a relationship with the chivalrous term 'taking a knee', which is respectfully bending down to one knee. This breaks the line of the leg and is also theatrically considered as 'taking a bow'. So saying 'break a leg' can be well wishes of a successful performance deserving many bows. Another thought is that it refers to keeping relaxed and loose. A little heads up reminder to bend one's knees slightly, avoiding nervous disasters of fainting from 'locked' knees under hot stage lights.

The first butterfly you see, cut off his head across your knee, bury the head under a stone and plenty of money will be your own.

If a dog sniffs a person's left knee it's an indication of gains with business, finance and/or service endeavors.

Ring 'good luck' into the New Year by toasting your champagne glasses loudly, wearing a cheery holiday knee garter and eating turnip greens.

In Thailand, dreams stricken with feelings of suffocation are attributed to sleeping cross-legged at the knees.

One is apt to be afflicted with illness if they perch removed shoes higher than their knees.

Placing the right garter and left shoe on first promotes good fortune.

Seeds sowed in the sign of the knee are sure to rot.

For old Scotts it was thought extremely 'unlucky' to sit with legs crossed at the knees while playing cards. Yet elsewhere this same situation is believed to have the opposite connotation-which is then realized as very lucky!

Hanging upside down by your knees is said to accelerate hair growth.

Should an ant crawl over one's left knee it's appreciated as a good omen.

The tenth house of the zodiac rules the knees.

Eastern European vampire folklore included a customary practice of cutting knee ligaments to prevent corpses from wondering around and returning from the dead.

A very destructive evil will suck your blood out if you continually lay down with one knee up.

To achieve invisibility one must obtain a dead man's patella bone from a cemetery at the stroke of midnight.

Ancient India had a ritual of drawing blood from the right knee, executed for approval from and in worship of their gods.

Green bark garters were worn as magical charms to protect against the powerful forces of maledictions.

Hunters of yore would snap a branch on their knee to fend off lurking evils. The sundered stick could also foretell bad break-poor hunt or lucky beak-good hunt.

Golfers can un-hex the curse of a bad swing by cracking a club over their knee.

It's a warning of pending treachery for the person whose garter has come undone.

In old Oregon if the right knee aches it's going to be stormy.

Jamaican folklore-if sugar cane is broken over the knee there will be a separation from a dear friend.

Losing a garter is coming trouble but if it is picked up and returned, anticipate help from a friend.

DREAM A LITTLE DREAM OF KNEE

Oneiromancy is the highly evolved method of assigning dream images with meanings. This divination attempts to clarify the intricate messages believed left behind as windows to our underlying self. These are commonly accepted age old interpretations;

DREAM IMAGE	MEANING
Ascending highlighting the knee, including going up stairs, ladders, ropes, escalators or hills	Success, increasing possibilities-
Descending downstairs, ladders, ropes, escalators or falling downward	Setbacks, reversals and failures-
Knees wearing jeweled garters	A lady's privacy will be betrayed and publicly exposed-
Knee garter(s) found	Indicating one is wearing themselves too thin, warning one will get burnt if they do not stop burning the candle at both ends-
Knee garter(s) lost	There will be un-expected treachery-
Knees are too large	Sudden bad luck-

Knee garters unfastened	A warning your associates are dangerous-
Knees in general	Unfortunate omens, flexibility, action capability to make progress, move ahead, humility, possible illness, dissatisfaction with home life, separation of lover, self doubts over-loaded, pride, ego, high emotional levels, in need of support, under pres-sure and being bullied-
Knee injured	A need to slow down and take stock-
Knees are shaky	Contemplated illicit intents will back fire-
Knees are stiff and painful	Fast and fearful danger awaits you-
Knees soiled	Illness foreseen-

Knee joints	Happiness for the future, changes for better, domestic joy and plenty of money junctions, bonding, connections and merging-
Kneeling	Agreement without questioning or in danger of being cheated-
Knees unshapely	Unhappy changes, dissolving hopes of love/ female-
Knees well formed and smooth	Will have a lot of male attentions but no marriage offers(f)

MOLEOSCOPY is a form of divination that assesses personality and futures from moles on the body;

General knee area	Careless indolent nature, selfish, lazy insensitive to others-
Left knee	A strong business mind, brash & ill- natured, grabby & extravagant, often regret- ful and inpatient, disagreeable confrontational, obstinate, uptight, rigid, no forethought, hasty in judgments, quick in temper yet honest & many children-

Right knee	Pleasant disposition, social, friendly and a happy marriage that smoothly passes without stresses or money problems, one who has no need to expect misfortunes-
A man w/mole on knee	Destine for wealth-
Two moles close together	Two marriages and/or two heavy affairs-

URTICARIAOMANCY are insights derived from itches;

General knee area	you will soon be kneeling in an unfamiliar church, you have jealous feelings towards someone- about to sleep in new bed-
Left knee	someone is gossiping about you- anticipate an unpleasant trip- fluttering is auspicious-
Right knee	there's good news for you, you're headed for pleasant travels- changes ahead-

BIRTH MARKS on a male's knees depicts he will marry a rich woman. When it's on a female's left knee as long as she remains good and forthright the future will prove fruitful.

MATRIMONY

A proper gentleman does his bidding 'hat in hand' and on 'bended knee'. Considered one of the most romantic deeds possible still only 20% of American men propose in this manner. A chivalrous gesture emanated from knighthood of yore. When knighted a subject is anointed one knee to ground pledging loyalty and the other up in ready servitude. Before tournaments, a knight would kneel awaiting his 'lady' to show favor with great pageantry by tossing him her colors or ribbons. Explorers dipped a knee as they claimed and flagged new territory, in name of their country or regal benefactors. Prince charming bowed his knee down to fit the glass slipper.

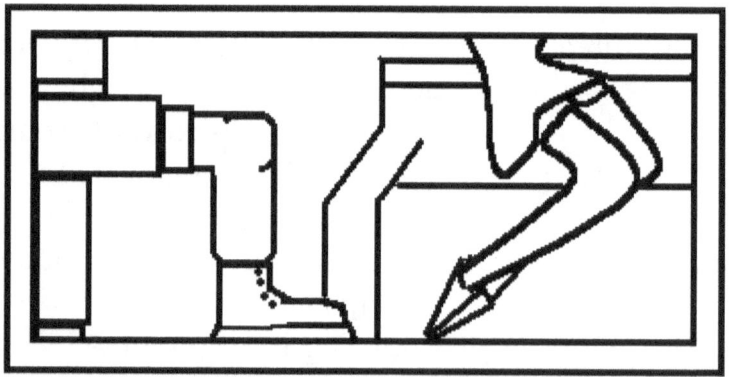

Known as an eldest of such alliances the 'Nobel Order of the Garter' was founded in 1348 by Edward III. It's rumored to have been initiated by a valiant effort to protect the dignity of a fair damsel who had lost her garter. This elite group of cavalier bluebloods is dedicated to the highest standards of gallantry. Only women of royalty can be invested, their regalia includes a blue (color of purity and fidelity) velvet garter worn below the left knee. It was enchantment that transcended special entitlement of a blue silk garter when wed, henceforth 'true blue' and 'queen for a day'.

No harm will befall the bride wearing a blue garter.

Hair to the knee never a bride will be.

A husband or suitor has been unfaithful if a girl loses her garter on the street.

To see your future husband in a dream hang a garter on the bedroom wall, point the toes of your shoes at right angles, say a little prayer and go to bed in silence.

When a girl loses her garter, a proposal of marriage is in the near future.

The man who caught the bridal garter wears it on his hat for good luck.

To reveal future mate the girl sleeps with a garter under her pillow, he will then appear in her dreams.

To increase chances of being married by the year's end single females needed to wear one yellow garter and one black garter on Easter Monday.

For a woman to ensure the love and hope of a man she should steal his hatband then wear it as her garter.

A young girl makes a parcel of 3 clay cuttings that have been tied in her left stocking with her right garter. By putting it under her pillow her dreams will reveal her future husband and fates.

A bride loosing a garter during her honeymoon is a bad omen for the union.

A garter sliding down while being worn means one's lover is thinking of them.

Loose a garter, loose a love.

To improve odds of happiness a kind-hearted girlfriend allows the bride to wear her garter.

If a man gives his sweetheart the garter of a new bride it guarantees her faithfulness for life.

A happily married woman gives a bride one of her garters (as in 'something old') to pass along the joy of her bliss.

A man getting a bride's garter is good luck and the catcher is thought to be next in line to wed.

For a lover to dream of finding his sweeties' garter means he will be confronted with many rivals and she will lose interest in him.

If a woman dreams of losing a garter her lover will act suspicious and jealous of others.

For a married man dreaming of a garter indicates his wife will discover his illicit ways with an unpleasant out come.

If a woman dreams of a paramour fastening her garters it signifies his undying loyalty and devotion.

Dream wearing a garter means seduction & amorous desire.

A garter lost and searched for signifies quarrels and marital bitterness.

Guest of 14th century European wedding festivities believed any piece of a bride's attire held good luck and fortune, most valued prize being the garter. Tying the knot was an occasion of great merriment but left a poor girl shredded and bruised. Eventually women voluntarily threw tokens or ribbons out with the coveted truss. Erstwhile it was thought when a groom removed the bridal garter it represented capturing her virginal girdle and relinquishing of virtue. That could explain the extreme conjugal band obsession. Sometimes intoxicated gents became so inpatient they would make obnoxious and crude attempts to acquire it. To avoid being accosted many resorted to holding male competitions of games or races. At some point, folks figured to keep peace it would work out best if a groom retrieved the garter and flung it to waiting lusty bachelors. Accommodating available females, his better half started throwing them her bouquet.

Hammers are protection talismans materializing from the Viking God Thor. One is placed between a bride's knees at her wedding for fertility, destruction, and power.

In old Ramoni-gypsy custom newlyweds sat encircled by their loving friends and family. A small measure of salt and bread was placed on the bride's knees. Next, the groom would take a portion, sprinkle it with some salt and then eat it. The bride would do the same thing. This union of hallah and salt symbolized completion of a harmonious bond.

Following several ceremonious exchanges, a Tibetan duo is ready to begin their hymeneal rites. Together they kneel in front of his uncle and a picture of Buddha while monks chant in the background. The new wife to be serves her future in-laws milky-tea flicking a fingertip salute of it upwards towards the heavens, honoring earth and Buddha.

Sungkem, performed in front of a gargoyle fountain, is a marriage ritual of Sudan. A united pair humbly bends forward and kisses the knees of their parents while asking for forgiveness and blessings. All the while, promising their everlasting duty and devotion to them.

After nuptials, some Chinese have an elaborate tea ceremony honoring the male's relatives and signifying early arrival of offspring. Together with assistance of a 'lucky woman', the young couple kneels in font of his parents while preparing and serving a special tea.

At the altar during vows in a very traditional German espousal, a groom kneels on a bride's gown letting it be known who will be 'wearing the pants'. As they stand, she in turn will stomp his foot showing which of them will have the 'last word'. You go girl!

Before the procession to church, all gather at a Polish bride's home. Here they partake in and witness lavish farewells. Of utmost importance is a blessing usually given by the maiden's mother. Presented as the intended twosome kneels on cushions hand in hand in font of their immediate elders, showered in brush sprinkler mist (a moistened branch suffices).

There is a Cajun practice with a spicy twist. A blushing bride sits on a best man's knee and/or lap while her new husband removes the garter, which he then flings over his shoulder to anxiously waiting single men.

Flash forward to modern America, the event prevails but behavior has tamed. You are not likely to see the grand cordon ripped off by the groom's teeth, it is more apt to be harmless under dress or sling shot antics. Nowadays they usually kneel down and gently use their hands while the bride is seated on a chair. In addition, there may be two worn just above the right knee, one for keepsake and one to toss.

MEDICINAL

It was preliterate elders who planted the seeds of healing practices. They intuitively staked out markers and perimeters of the human condition. Then delved into native surroundings and cultivated attributes to suit needs of the community. Social terrains broadened and rudimentary offshoots crowded the contour for centuries. The supporting foray was dominated by a myriad of arthritic and rheumatoid curatives.

With the infiltration of scientific research, procedures strayed from the folk attitude. Many remedies coincided with the results of medical studies but were discounted. Despite the obstacles of period controversies, several treatments managed to keep their properties intact. So much so, that two-thirds of the world population continues to rely on herbal medications.

A third of American adults have tried a non-conventional option, that's only the ones admitting to it. Did they forget about tiger balm in their gym bag to rub on sore knees, how they press on a side of their kneecap to relieve pressure, or the lotus position learned at camp to calm their system? Perhaps these methods are so prevalent they do not automatically register as non-prescribed. Maybe that's what was available, affordable at the time and it worked!

Due to mounting interest in total well-being and a constant rise in insurance cost, rigid professionals have chosen to adopt 'new' healthcare approaches. Known as CAM (complementary alternative medicine) therapies, their course is in conjunction with standard medicine. These fresh looks are performed without the acknowledgement of age-old benefits or merited support. Once considered 'backwoods' thinking it is evident the fundamental roots never really lost their foothold.

GENERAL-MAINLY PERTAINING TO ARTHRITIS, RHEUMATISM, PAIN AND SWELLING

KNEE AILMENT PROTECTION CHARMS;
Lucky rabbit's foot-
Carry buckeye or nutmeg in either side of pocket-
Wearing a sprig of Rowan or Mountain Ash tree-
Turtledoves nesting near home-
Wearing cast off snake skin-
Wearing knuckle bones-
Shell necklace with spider inside-
Wearing a dime around ankle prevents arthritis-
Keeping finger & toenails trimmed-
While in bed, keep a bar of soap in nylon stocking-
Wear socks all of the time-

KNEE AILMENT TREATMENTS;
Cat's claw-
Willow tree tea-
Carrying buckeye-
Bee stings-
Goose grease mixed with turpentine-
Press cobwebs on affected area-
Devil's claw-
Rub on olive oil-
Apply mashed peyote-
Drink wine laced with ground ivy-
Bury aching joint-
Soak in temascal-
Rub legs with greasy towels-
Eat soy beans-
Melted dog fat-
Boiled seaweed-
DMSO (80's industrial solvent sold curbside)-

KNEE CRAMP CURES;
Black ribbon under knees-
Carry graveyard patella-
Sleeping with a mole skin-
Stems of periwinkle tied around knees-
Carry human skull-
Wear red ribbon of silk under knees-
Sport cork garters-
Wrap with red kerchief-
With just the toes sticking out put shoes under coverlet-
Carry patella of sheep leg or wear sheep kneecap-
Hold human patella bone-
Wearing eel garters-
Tote about patella of a baby lamb-
Put cold water behind the knee-
Tie candlewick around leg just below knee-
Wear wide rubber band above knee w/dime underneath-
Rub turpentine on stomach with flannel & lift knees to chin-

KNEE GOUT REMEDIES;
Apply very hot-bagged anthill poultice to scare away gout-
Digest horse/ant oil-
Put on right sock first in morning-
Eat juniper berries-
Ingest sugar of lead-
Pack in ox dung-
Sleep with bowl of turpentine & water under bed-
Apply snakes around joints-
Bandage with right foot of frog in deer skin-
Eel salve-
Rub with fresh cut ginger-
Seal in cabbage, plastic wrap than a towel-
Eat fresh strawberries-
Black cherry juice-

Egg and brandy plaster-
Watered down black strap molasses-
Teaspoon of baking soda before meals-
For males increased sexual activity-
Spinach, spinach and more spinach-
Potassium-
Bananas-
Alfalfa sprouts-
Bilberry-
Celery juice-
Activated charcoal daily-
Parsley-
Hawthorn-
Apply vinegar boiled mullein leaves-
Grapes-
1/2 Yarrow & ½ sting nettles cooled tea-
Black cohash-
Buchu tea-
Blueberries-
Gravelroot-
Pine bark and grape seed extracts-
Devil's claw-
Sack area w/birch leaves 1-2hrs daily-
Steeped horse radish juice for 10 days-
Tissue salts-
Corncob tea-
Wear Sapphire charm-
Rub on sugared stewed ants-
Pack between 2 loafs of uncut bread-
Wrap in deerskin with legless spider-
Rub on mixture of cow manure & goat milk butter-
Have your horse stand in the creek-
Make plaster of mule urine with wax & oil-
Tie knot in highest shoot of pine tree-

Eat ground ivy-
Soak in snail water-
Digest salted owl with boar's grease-
Dress area with rabbit's lard-
Rub on deer marrow-
Eat ripe cherries-
Crush snails & apply the paste-
Rub with peppermint oil-
Eat holly leaves-
Massage with rose oil-
Apply dove buttocks-
Cover in hot hen dung-
Bath in urine-
Eat turnips-
Apply boiled rosemary-
Wear coral charm necklace-
Burn live ravens-
Eat bread with dove blood-
Dress area with raw beef-
Digest raven ashes-
Ceragem-Korean CAM circulation & massage therapy-
Wrap in cooked cabbage-
Drink vinegar & honey-
Stroke area with corpse bone-
Leek plasters-
Own & care for a turtledove-
Drink gopher grass tea with turpentine-
Allow spiders to breed in home-
Wrap in flesh of goose hawk-
Apply gull's grease-
Rub on hare's blood-
Apply turkey vulture fat-
During funeral, throw 77 grains of salt in body of water-
Eat endive seeds-

Walk in open fields before sunrise on Fridays-
Honeysuckle suave-
Sleep with puppies-
Grind moss & apply-
Drink water from the juncture of 2 rivers-
Wrap in eagle flesh-
Rub with cucumber-
Consume alligator flesh-
Gout stool (medical quackery)-

ARTHRITIS REMEDIES;
Drink rosemary tea-
Consume sesame seeds-
Eat oregano-
Mustard plasters-
Red or Cayenne pepper for pain relief internally & topically-
Keep a Chihuahua-
Wear the rings of dead people-
Carry buckeye tree seeds-
Apply heated stones & bricks-
Rub joints with whisky-
Drink uranium ore wash water-
Eat gallbladder of live serpent-
Rub silver dollar over joint-
Corn mash moonshine-
Sweat and steam baths-
Wear ashes inside stockings-
Rub with fox pelt-
Sawdust of cedar tree in shoe-
Whale blubber internally and topically-
Alfalfa tea-
Eat raven brain-
Ingest horse hoof that has been boiled-
Rub with skunk skin-

Inhale air from uranium mine-
Cross-garter in wet red flannel-
Carry hickory nut in back pocket-
Eat green apple cores-
Paint knees with molasses/creosote mix after ½ hour remove
  with kerosene-
Spells of transferring to another life force (to plant, animal
  or person)-
Wear chains of brass-
Marijuana tea-
Digest garlic-
Microwave a rice-filled sock and apply for relief-
Puncture joint-
Drink one's own urine-
Ingest beans and papayas together-
Apply paste made from a handful of sea salt-
Sleeve in shark skin-
Consume numerous pills such as aspirin-
Soak in natural or hot springs-
Apply holly spray-
Eat bread-baked earthworms-
Don gold jewelry-
Rub on minced garlic-
Horse chestnuts under mattress-
Soak in Epsom salts-
Drink all the milk you can hold-
Eat whiskey soaked raisins-
Rub on dirty dish water-
Sulphur & molasses tonic-
Ingest herbs & roots mixed with whiskey-
Patented snake oils-
Wear rings with cutout crosses-
Chew honeycomb-
Mixture of alcohol & marijuana rub-

Heals of shoes put up against wall-
Pennies in shoes-
Rub on oil of earthworm-
Absorb radiation-
Wear rings forged from coins without thanking benefactors-
Rub on sauerkraut juice-
Chew wild cherry bark-
In dark room, rub joints with copper penny-
Put course salt and cornmeal in shoes-
Drink grated potato juice-
Wear the sign of Capricorn-
Coat in rotten cheese-
Mineral oil rubs-
Consume lemon & honey-
Spraying WD-40 on knees provides pain relief & increased
  mobility (from a Reader's Digest publication)-
Wear rings forged from coffin handles-
Childbirth-
Rub with corn cooking oil-
Apply fresh chicken blood-
Bind knees in hot steamed towels-
Apply vinegar soaked brown paper-
Cake with red mud-
Feed on pigeon pot pies-
Carry slice of raw potato-
Drink lemon juice with white egg in it-
Apply swamp weed-
Drink juice from boiled grapefruit rind-
Point to a star & then bite finger-
Ingest dog meat-
Eat white area of orange-
Drink other people's urine-
Eat fresh snake flesh-
Apply goat milk-

Mud baths-
Apply potato peelings-
Peppermint oil massage-
Rub on fish worm oil-
Consume rhubarb powder-
Sleep with dog or cat at foot of bed-
Bee sting on heal of same leg affected-
Rub in mixture of white gasoline & salt-
Cod liver oil-
Tiger balm-
Wrap In fresh salmon-
Hog head bone worn on string around neck-
Rub in a blister causing ointment-
Stay buried to waist overnight-
Wear chicken feather in bag around neck-
Sleep with snake in feed sack-
Consume a ripe pokeberry for 9 days, cease for 9 days &
  repeat-
Brush knees with wild bore bristles-
Aroma therapy-
Rub on mixture of 1-pint vinegar, 1-pint turpentine & 2 eggs
Pack in yellow dirt made like dough-
Sprinkle on spunk water (water collected from well of
  hallow tree stump)-
Twirl dead cat overhead in woods, toss north walk away &
  don't look back-
Vinegar with the mother (non-pasteurized), the milky
  residue floating on top-
Drink green tea-
Rub on fence slat that hogs have scratched against-
Wear garnets-
Heat seaweed on iron grill then tie in place & bandage-
Float or wade in Soap Lake-
Magnets-

RHEUMATISM REMEDIES;
Apply oakum, honey and vinegar-
Own a Chihuahua-
Sip liquid gold tea-
Brick dust doorway thresholds-
Consume mixture of bear grease, groundhog grease, pepper
  and nutmeg-
Heated rattle snake oil rub on knees-
Wear a horseshoe ring-
Rub dried turkey wishbone all over knees then burn bone-
Wear copper bracelets-
Apply skunk grease to knees-
Place hop filled pillow under bed-
Put dried mustard in shoes-
Tea laced with chimney soot-
Wear brass ring on forefinger-
Squeal while rubbing on tree where hogs rubbed-
Early 1900's physicians implanted $5 gold pieces near joint-
Rattlesnake belt-
Smear knees w/Vick's Vapor Rub then seal in plastic wrap-
Drink first voided urine of day-
Burn buzzard feathers-
Put left sock on first daily-
Carry knucklebone of pig in pocket-
Rub knees with pork that has been read over in prayer-
Hydrotherapy-
Let cat lick knees
Mink oil-
Plant seedling with animal placenta-
Bath in heated rainwater with rose hips-
Supper and socialize with elders-
Tie locket of hair in tree hollow-
Rub area with sour apple cores-
Suck honey out of wild purple clovers-

Wrap in fox pelts-
Jimson weed wrap-
Cross shoes at night-
Drink sage tea-
Carry 5 chestnuts in pant's pocket-
Walk barefoot over fresh dirt-
Carry right hind paw of squirrel-
Pebble in pocket-
Rub with ashes of mouse baked alive-
Sulphur in shoes-
Hold cat in lap-
Eat pokeberries-
Kill buzzard bury for 3 days dig up and pluck all feathers off
Potato in bra-
Continually soak feet in very hot water-
Wear red flannel under garments-
Consume Gordon's gin and anise seed-
Crack fresh ostrich egg over knees and let dry-
Press spider webs on knees-
Ride to church in buggy borrowed from vicar-
Whitewash knees-
Rub joint with ivory tusk of an elephant-
Sprinkle white pepper over knees-
Carry penny that has been flattened on railroad tacks-
Rub area with back of chilled silver spoon-
Wish on a falling star-
Put copper plates in shoes-
Deviled eggs-
Drink dissolved gelatin-
Fan with dry ferns-
Joint rotation therapy-
Rub mirrors on knees to attract energy from the sun-
Mustard greens-
Place lizard in earthenware pot for 20 days-

Wear a ten-penny nail ring-
Bathe where ice has been broken through in a stream-
Rub on black hen blood-
Carry the rattles of rattlesnakes-
Drink hot lemon juice-
Wear black bill Indian duck feathers-
Ingest tincture of cat-
Keep ring neck doves in home-
Consume oil of wintergreen mixed with sugar-
Wear front paw of mole dangling on cotton string-
Dime around neck-
Wear copper soled socks (filaments embedded in yarn)-
Swallow baby nail clippings for gold content-
Rub on alligator fat-
Sit in the wind of burning cow pies-
Beet & mustard greens poultice-
Walk in mashed cow manure-
Steel rings-
Soak in fish barrel-
Marijuana brownies-
Wear nutmeg around neck & nibble for 9 days-
Brass ring on middle finger of left hand-
Drink whiskey in which dried rattlesnake skin has soaked-
Chamomile tea gathered before sunset of St. John's Eve-
Apply dog grease-
Hide chestnuts in clothing-
Soak in mineral waters from St. Louis Michigan-
Walk in the dew-soaked tall grasses-
Drink green gourd water-
Birth year penny in the shoe-
Cover with elm tree leaves while lying on ground-
Drink water that has dripped from the grapevine-
Magnets-
Wrap red yarn around knee-

Sleep on feathers-
Zimmer Gender High-Flex Knee-(female replacement)
Potato in sock-
Bury money-
Put bills in shoes under feet-
Suck on ivory or bone buttons-
Wade in creek by light of blue moon-
Have a little red haired girl deliver your eggs-
Plant tree with a prayer-
Suck on copper penny-
A & D ointment-
Burn old leather shoes-
Wrap in nettle tea soaked cheesecloth-
Yoga and meditation-
Rub knees with ash of burnt stump-
Spit on shoes and put them under your bed-
Yogurt, internally and externally-
Potato pancakes-
Horsemint tea-
Rub with mink pelts-
Soak feet in detox-spa 1/2hr. daily-
Boiled and salted gourd water-
Pack in mashed turkey giblets-
Sleep on bed of ferns-
Stroll to the river naked & bathe-
Rub hand of a dead corpse on area-
Bury bottle of water that contains your fingernail clippings-
Wear a sack full of live bees-
Polecat grease-
Chicken fat-
Hemp seed oil-
Whiskey soaked pokeberry root-
Smoke of dried flowers fanned over knees-
Rub with wash water of petrified wood-

Let waterfall run over and saturate knees-
Wear plaster of rotten cheese-
Cut open fresh rabbits on knees-
Indian turnip carried in pocket-
Place shoes upside down beneath bed-
Stolen potato from field of neighbor-
Carry unripe walnuts-
Lye plasters-
Sleep in a room in which several rabbits roamed about-
Put stolen apple in pocket-
Wrap with cloth soaked in one's own menstrual blood-
Red potato in trousers pocket-
Wear brass in one toe and steel in the other-
Rub on paste of elder flowers & fruits-
Sleep on mattress with corks in it-
Duct tape bands beneath caps of aching (football) knees-
Wear chicken wishbone around neck-
Sew potato into slip-
Go near beeswax (gum) & get severely sting-
Rub on clay & buttermilk mixture-
Wear cloth bandages soaked in one's own urine-
Carry double cedar knot in pocket-
Purge grass & lion's tongue-
Bleed old chicken on knees-
Oil of wild cat killed & buried for 4 days-
Horseradish plasters-
Wrap in mullein leaves-
Drink tonic of sweet spirits of nitrate, Epson salts, lemon
  & cold water-
Rattle tied with string-
Where the affected joint rest put a razor under bed sheet-
Dried up potato in bed-
Wear shoulder bone of black feline-
Rub 3 times the head of a golden haired tot-

Rye straw smoke-
Carry roundest bone of a ham joint-
Sleep with pan of nails under bed-
Wear hazelnuts-
For 10 nights, walk over graveyard dirt-
Buzzard's feather stuck in hatband-
Wear ring shaped from potato-
Rub baby's head3 times after touching painful spot with
  same hand-
Carry aged haddock bone-
Trace charcoal crosses on both knees-
Clip fingernails on Friday-
Wear sealing wax stroked red flannel-
Pat the head of a little blond girl 3 times in light of moon-
Place peppercorns under bed at night-
Keep shoes upside down in the evening-
For 3 full days, do not comb hair-
Wear wristband of cork or leather-
Jump across 7 river rocks in a row without falling in-
Apply hornet's nest-
Acorn necklace-
Have child who has never seen their father walk on your
  back-
Spit on a rock then hide it under the front porch
Burn your hair clippings-
Put crushed nuts in toe of both shoes-
Cat blood soaked red flannel wraps-
Stepping over the dog house-
Wear dried eel skins-
Put glass knobs under bed post-
Apply grape skins-
Branding or tattooing-
Apply angle worms-
Rub on camphor-

Buzzard's feather behind ear-
Drink gardener snake oil-
Apply mixture of mashed angleworms, goose & hog grease-
Drink wine in which an iron nail has soaked-
Sleep with uranium under bed-
Carry a dime wrapped in red flannel-
Wear nutmeg and powdered clove in both shoes-
In morning, wash face before hands-
Wear wide or doubled leather belt-
Apply snake fat-
Always put right shoe on first-
Bury your toe nails-
Encourage insect stings and bites-
Put Friday nail clipping in jar of water or brandy & place
  under bed-
Australians mend knees with a sticky substance in frog skin-
Wrap knee in unwashed sheep's wool-
Carry goat knuckle bone-
Wear nine times dyed flannel shirt-
Drink juice of grated potato-
Wear symbol of the sign of Capricorn-
Alcohol bath then wrap knees in white linen-
Mineral oil massage-
Chew raw potato-
Apply 3 & 1 oil-
Beet leaves plaster-
Nasturtium salad-
Coat knees with wild dog saliva-
Bury knee 2 hours in church yard-
Eat alfalfa seeds-
Apply boiled potatoes-
Cod liver oil-
Horse chestnuts under bed-
Indian root-

Every other week sulphur in shoes-
Wrap with bandage that has a live toad in it-
Drink red oak bark tea-
Apply blood from mole-
Rub on baked buzzard grease-
Mothball in pocket-
Apply whiskey soaked snake-
Bathe in boiled cedar leaves-
Stroll in crushed cow manure-
Dry cupping, inverting cup in which the inside air is heated
  causing a vacuum-
Recline on ground covered in elm tree leaves-
Bind live frog to back-
Apply alligator flesh-
Bathe in oats-
Apply paste of daises & butter-
Paint area with vinegar-
Coat in red iodine-
Wear copper pennies that had been on eyelids of corpse-
Sleep with guinea pig in bed-
Apply panther oil-
Sleep with head north & feet south-
Hang holed stone from earth over bed-
Put urine in hog bladder then keep it in a constant burning
  fire chimney for 3 days-
Mush on rotten apples-
Carry frozen raw potato-
Don ring made from a horse shoe-
Carry eyetooth of hog-
Rheumatism chairs peddled by charlatans of the Louis XVI
  period-
Rabbit brush tea-
Put hair & nail clippings into a drilled elder-tree hole
  wedging with plug (plugging)-

Tractor therapy major fad of 1776, Dr. Perkins sold
   metal rods he claimed to draw out aliments-
Drink dandelion wine or dandelion tea-
Apply peanut oil-
Electric bells strapped around knees for vibrations (medical
   quackery)-
Kneel amongst fresh mint leaves-
Apply hard dry horse dung-
Sniff skinned raw herring-
Drink a mixture of garlic, powdered brimstone, whisky and
   saltpeter (yuk!) -
Wolf grease-
Paraffin wax coating (melt & cool just so it won't burn then
   dip or pour, allow to cool)-
Battery & metal disc charges (medical quackery)-
Slice open fresh duck across knees-
Rub on mixture of garlic & animal dung-
Leech therapy (pilot studies are again being suggested)-
Consume yellow catfish fat oil-
Wrap in flesh of cow killed by lightning-
When removing shoes turn tops in, put under bed & speak to
   no one for rest of the night-
Ritual performed over knees by third generation carpenter-
Allow piglets, puppies, or kittens to suckle on swollen joints
Wet kerchief in distant forest spring-
Touch affected area to a hole made in tree & fill with sand-
Boiled lion's paw-
Rub in mixture of boiled human urine, salt, ashes & spirits-
Apply urgent of coal oil, camphor gum & kerosene-
Eat pickles-
Wet cupping; a scarificator cuts the knee and uses cups to
   suction and contained the blood-
The Oxford partial knee-
Burnt toast and butter tea-

KNEE INFLAMMATION;
Eat pineapple-
Wrap in a minced onion paste overnight-
Apply ointment of fried snails-
Put warm fresh cow manure on knees-
Sudden shock therapy by firing shot gun placed under knees
Blanket with steaming corn husk-
Apply Jimson weed poultice-
Acupressure-
Ice at twenty-minute intervals-

KNEE AILMENT CURES;
Carrying an old blacken potato in your pocket-
Bryony like mandrake-
Rubbing area with the yellow meat of a turtle-
Chestnut shell garters-
Crawling through an archway made of bramble-
Bathing before daybreak on Easter day-
Hazel tree-
Tote about ashes of dead toad-
Crushed red pepper poultice-
Tie red string around affected areas-
Red ribbon garters-
Be buried naked in a churchyard-
Keep right foot of a hare with you-
Wearing a ring made from the metal of an old coffin-
Carrots, carrots and more carrots-
Carrying an elder tied in knots in your pocket-
Swallow garlic whole-

BOW-LEGGED TREATMENTS
Pound a nail into an oak tree-
One must sleep with legs wrapped around a rain barrel-
Sweep down back of knees with sedge broom-
Bite from the ground the first fern that appears in springtime

CAUSES OF KNEE JOINT AILMENTS;
Eating too rich of foods (poor diet) & lack of exercise-
Bearing excessive weight-
Smoking-
Burning meal bones in a fire-
High heel shoes-
Kicking a cat-
Cold & damp temperatures-
Curses, spells, demons or angry spirits-
Hereditary-

SKINNED KNEES-(plus grass and rug burns)
Butterfly kisses (flutter eyelashes on ouie)-
Kissing the boo-boo by MOM- good old fashioned TLC-
Shave cream (urban)-
Make frozen compresses with water filled colorful balloons-
Brown wash cloths (hides any blood)-
Frozen fun sponges, refreshing & numbing-
Red iodine (old school)-
Honey and lard ointment-
Brown soap and sugar paste-
Marigold cream-
Aloe Vera or Tea tree oil-
Use inner layer of a raw eggshell as bandage-
Apply inside of a banana to knee, promotes healing-
Wash with weak solution of baking soda-
Crushed plantain leaf on scraped or bleeding knee-
Ease pain by rubbing abrasion with crushed basil leaves-
Wash wound well then sprinkle pepper on to scrape-
Sprinkle cinnamon on clean wound-
Clean w/lemon then dip into powdered cloves-
Newspapers stuffed in plastic bags protect housework knees-
For darkened knees rub with lime juice & 1 tspn coconut oil-
Pineapple skins scrub down-

OTHER FOLK REMEDIES

Appendicitis:
On hands and knees, slide downstairs-preventative-

Backache:
Have someone knee on your back-

Blackheads:
Crawling & creeping under brambles-
Crawl 3 times & creep sun wise through natural tree
bramble arch-
Crawl & sneak on hands & knees through bramble 3 times
from east to west-

Boils:
String nutmeg around knee -
While fasting creep on hands and knees beneath bramble-
Creep-crawl through natural bramble at sunrise three times-
Crawl through bramble with both ends grown into the soil-

Brittle elderly bones:
Wear basswood knee splints-

Chest ailments:
Lick salt from shoulders & knees in diagonal pattern-
Laying on back bring knees to chest repeatedly-

Childbirth, delivery & labor:
Sit on man's knees-
Sit astride husband's knees-
During delivery man knees the small of woman's back-
Kneeling labor, hold onto sheet hanging from ceiling-
If the husband ties her garters, the mother to be will give
birth easily-

Chills:
On knees go down a flight of stairs head first 3 times-

Colds:
Rub lard on knees then wrap-

Colic:
Place person on stomach & put knees in small of back-
Put baby across knees & pat their back-

Constipation:
While sitting on toilet bang & smack knees-
Crawling around on floor-
Crawl around table of dinning room floor-

Eyes:
On knees go westward 9 times around Mary's well followed
by drinking 1 cup of water Circumambulation-
Close eyes and rest up against knees-

Female ailments:
Wear cloth bandages soaked in one's own urine-
Wrap with cloth soaked in one's own menstrual blood-
Perfume behind knees for birth control-
Paint knees with menstrual blood-
To slow flow paint around knees with bluing-

Fever:
Apply black chicken meat to back of knees-

Hiccups:
While laying on back hold knees-
Hang upside down by knees-
Put head between knees-
With head between knees, tap head 3 times with knees-

Insects, bedbugs & jiggers:
Tie kerosene soaked string below knee-
Tie red yarn under knees-

Intellect:
Head between knees inhale & exhale as fast as possible
(brain breathing to increase oxygen for smarts)-
Hang upside down by your knees-

Liver ailments:
Crawl under table till you laugh & shake impurities loose-

Neck pain:
On knees rub up to area where hogs have rubbed-

Nosebleed:
Hold head between knees-

Nursing, weaning:
Wean babies in the sign of the knee-
Wean baby when the sign is below the knees-
Wean when sign runs out, (tenth house of zodiac)-

Side aches:
Kiss knee opposite side of ache-

Sterility:
Walk 3 times around church on knees with a white ram-

Stomach ache:
Crawl from east to west & north to south under dinning
room table-
Apply hot moist turpentine to stomach & lift knees to chin-
Kneeling next to wild thyme bite off 3 leaves massage them
behind knees-

<u>Talking speaking</u>:
Apply jumped-up butter crumbs to knees (crumbs flowing
on surface of skim-milk)-
Breath deep and blow on knees-

<u>Teeth</u>:
Teeth should be pulled when the sign is below the knee-
Toothache-put bowl of oats on head kneel beside body then
throw oats into water-
To keep from gagging in the dentist chair raise right leg
above your left knee as fast as possible-

<u>Walking</u>:
Apply jumped-up butter crumbs to back of knees-
Rub down knees with dirty dish water-
Cut head of live turtle & rub child's knees w/blood-
To encourage a child's walking broom back of knees-
Tickle little one's on back of knees-

During the depression, Great Grandma Billie ended up
having a no-nonsense farm wife life. True to her character,
she became proficient in resourcefulness while mastering
reliable cleaning and health concoctions. There is no
memory of her ever being afflicted but it was grandma and
she swore the following recipe relieves the pain of arthritis:

Ingredients: gin and <u>golden</u> raisins.

Put the raisins into a bowl then pour in just
enough gin to completely cover them. Let
the alcohol evaporate (it takes about a week)
then store plumped raisins in a lidded glass
jar. Eat nine of the prepared raisins daily.

She had them on oatmeal.

KNEE LANGUAGE

LANGUAGE	TRANSLATION
Afrikaans	knie
Albanian	gju
Cataian	genoll
Danish	knae
Double Dutch	kuknunee
Eggy-Peggy	kneggeegge
Dutch	knie
English (old English)	cneo
Esperanto	genuo
Finnish	polvi
French	genou
Frisian	knibble
German	knie
Hungarian	térd
I-ing	knii
Italian	ginocchio
Latin	genu; popies
Malay	lutut
Na	kneeena
Norwegian	kne
Papiamento	rudia
Pig Latin	ee-knay
Polish	kolano
Portuguese	joelho
Romanian	genunchi
Scottish Gaeli	glùn
Spanish	rodilla
Sranan	kindi
Swahili	goti
Swedish	knä

110

Tagalog	túhod
Thief-Language	koknonee
Turkish	diz
Ubbi Dubbi	knubee
Yiddish	kni
Yucatec	piix

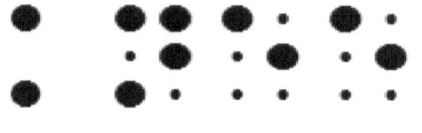

BRAILLE

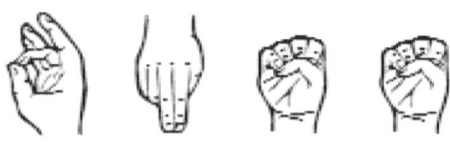

MORSE CODE

HAND
SIGN LANGUAGE

膝

CHINESE

무릎

KOREAN

Body Talk

60% of human communication is non-verbal. Every culture has a unique physical vocabulary. Sign Language is a perfect example: pointing to the knee(s) indicates knee(s). If a Modern Greek places his left hand on his knee, closing one eye, looking up with the other into a middle distance, then wags a free hand up and down; it means "I don't want anything to do with it." In ancient Egypt when young men came across acquaintances they would salute (greet) with the hand hanging along side of their knee. These particular body behaviors are fairly obvious whereas most are subtle or subconscious.

Knee pointing is when a foot is tucked under the opposite thigh. This tends to be an informal female position where a knee aims in the direction of an interesting prospect. Slowly crossing or uncrossing legs, slightly stroking her knee, kicking the top leg back and forth plus dangling a shoe are strong attraction signals. If she's blocking her lap this is a protective move or an intended deterrent. It's never proper for princesses to cross their lower limbs in public. Causing commotion flappers raised eyebrows with just a glimpse of their gartered knees. Flashing a bit of naked knee is always a sweet slice of cheesecake.

A figure-four (ankle on opposite knee) displays the crotch and is considered a male seating position. If their hand then rest on the calf or knee he is bracing himself. Crossing legs with one on the other knee has been known as a gang sign of impending retribution.

A man gently placing his hand on a lady's knee has sexual innuendos. If he puts it between her knees, he's likely to get smacked and 'cut off at the knees'. If a woman puts her hand on a male knee it is encouragement, betwixt the knees he thinks it's an open invitation. Playing kneesies under the table implies innocent flirtation and there's a quiet intimacy sitting with knees touching side to side.

Dealing knee to knee suggests directness. Tapping your knee conveys an element of impatience. Plucking dust from your knees real or imaginary hints of mistrust to boredom. When trying to bring attention to something on the sly a little knee nudge works. A nasty knee bump in your bum while your shoulders are held back bluntly sends you down the road. Out of respect, knees should be together in church pews. Crawling while clinging to someone's knees portrays begging. Kneeling during prayer depicts reverence. Dropping to your knees and kissing the ground is true gratitude.

In our country being relaxed and comfortable is the primary goal often side stepping manners, it may simply be habit or totally unconscious. This laid back demeanor and presence reflects the American style as lazy and rude. Protocol is tighter elsewhere therefore never cross your legs in Thailand it's indecent especially with elders. English and French value politeness finding it proper to sit with knees together or with legs crossed at the knee. In Russia, crossing one's legs or placing a foot on one knee is thought inconsiderate.

There are hundreds of thousands distinct elementary gestures our bodies can perform. Although every situation is different and interpretations can vary all of these knee experiences have a meaning without making a sound. Knees have their own voice!

JOKES

When the boy broke his knee, where did he go to get a new one?
At the butcher's shop, where they sell kid-knees!

What kind of fish swims in the ocean and has two knees?
A two-knee (tuna) fish!

IPSO FACTO: There is no official single word in English for back of the knee.

TERMS

Ankylophobia	-fear of knee joint immobility
Bow legged	-bowed legs so knees don't touch
Bum knee	-a joint that isn't always hopping
Buckled knees	-unexpected collapsing of knees
Capped	-having knee caps smashed or death
Catapedaphobia	-fear of jumping from high and/or low places
Cock Knee Stone	-lucky pebble found in a cock's knee
Crawl	-creep on hands & knees
Curtsey	-dainty female knee dipping
Curve of the knee	-computer measurement
Cypress Knees	-knee-like Cypress tree roots under boardwalks or marshes
Deep knee bend	-closer to the floor squatting exercise
Dodgy knees	-tricky knees
Fatty Knees	-solidly built dingy
Geniculated	-knee like intergrowths of crystals
Genu valgum	-medical term for 'knock knees'
Genuflect	-to kneel
Genuflection	-act of bending knees in worship
Genuologist	-one well versed in the traits of knee features
Genuology	-science of defining knee traits
Genuphobia	-fear of knees
Ginglymoid	-knee hinge joint
Glass knee	-similar to glass jaw (shatters easy)
Golden Knee	-tarantula (Chaco)
Goosestep	-to march sharply with knees locked and rigid
High knee	-outdated lingo for upper crust

H-maid's knees	-bursitis discomfort caused by constant kneeling
Inknee (d)	-knock-kneed
JKS	-Jealous Knee Syndrome (envy)
Knack kneed	-knock-kneed
Knee	-joint between thigh & low leg
Knee	-specific clothing covering a knee
Knee	-knee like bend in pipe or wood
Knee basher	-baseball bat
Knee beam	-loom tool to move material & protect weaver's knee
Knee bend(s)	-squatting position exercise
Knee brush	-thick hair on bee's legs to aid collection of pollen
Knee buckle	-ornate or utility boot fasteners
Kneecap	-patella
Knee capper	-one who shoots or smashes the knees
Knee deep	-shallow or up to knee level
Knees dip/ (ping)	-to lower or set down one knee
Knee drill	-exercise program to procure proper technique & form
Knee drum	-drums between knees (bongos)
Knee harp	-small Irish harp held with knees
Knee hi(s)	-knee socks
Knee high	-reaches as high as knees
Knee highs	-socks up to knee
Kneehole	-desk with knee space cut out
Knee hugs	-kid's hugs for tall people
Knee jerk reaction	-instant unavoidable reaction
Knee jerk	-that 50 mil sec reflex reaction when the doctor mallets knee cap
Knee mill	-geared like the old time hand coffee grinder

Knee mouse	-particle(s) of free floating cartilage in knee joint
Knee of the Nile	-most fertile curve of the river
Knee of the road	-bend of the road
Knee pad	-cushioned patella protection
Knee pan	-patella
Knee pedal	-knee activated levers for mechanical operations
Knee pillow	-long cushion placed between knees during sleep or rest
Knee Pushups	-girl pushups with bent knees
Knee shimmy	-fancy belly dancing movement
Knee socks	-socks up to knee called knee hi-s
Knee timber	-timber with knee shaped angles
Knee tribute	-hailing humbled adoration on bended knees
Knee whacker	-sharp rap on knees or one that intently smacks them
Kneebar	-leg lock that hyper extends knee (wrestling)
Kneecapped	-enemy punishment of bursting or shooting kneecaps off
Knee crooking	-cringing; fawning
Kneed	-having knees or being struck by a knee
Kneeing	-striking with the knee
Kneeker	-type of knee warmer
Kneel(ing)	-support one self on the knees
Kneeler	-a board used for kneeling
Knee-mail	-praying messages to god
Kneemaology	-fear of knees bending back
Kneemaphobia	-fear of knees bending back
Kneeology	-school and power of prayer

Kneeroll	-English saddle supportive pad for rider's knee
Kneesies	-rub knees amorously w/another
Kneeskin	-advanced Lycra slick swimwear
Knee-slapper	-funny joke, line or story
Kneewall	-short wall construction or computers
Knobby knees	-boney protruding knee joints
Knock kneed	-bowed so that the knees touch
Knop-kneed	-knees bent inward from strain of bearing excessive weight
Kowtow	-to humbly genuflect
Nubby knees	-female unshaven knee area
Nub-Nub Soclings	-bits of color convertible knee-hi's
Patella	-ancient Roman dish or pan
Patella	-the kneecap
Patellae	-patella in plural
Red Knee	-tarantula (Mexican)
Rheo Knee	-2005's bionic knee replacement
Salaam	-to kneel in reverence
Scaping	-deep bow with foot drawn back
Secretary's knee	-chronic discomfort from prolonged bent position
Short Knees	-colorful carnival like skits/plays
Stifle	-knee
Stifle bone	-a small bone at the knee joint
Stripe Knee	-tarantula (Central American)
Thick knees	-type of bird
Trick knee	-knee that unexpectedly gives out
Weak in the knees	-unstable love struck feeling
Weak kneed	-cowardly, lacking will power
White Knee	-tarantula (Brazilian)
Wobbly knees	-shaky
Yellow Flame Knee	-tarantula (Mexican)

SLANG

AMERICAN:

Baker's knee	-knees bent inwards by carrying breadbaskets
Bee's knees	-height of perfection
Bow & scrape	-dipping of knee
Cold as a miner's knee	-cold
Cold as a well digger's knee	-cold
Cut off at the knees	-stop or nip in the bud
Dizz-knee-land	-juvenile detention
Hard as a goat's knee	-hard
Hotter than a preacher's knee	-hot (Deep-South)
Knee action	-front wheel auto suspension system (urban)
Knee bag	-nasty name calling (urban)
Knee-bender	-negative name for flatterer
Knee capping	-shooting out one's knees
2 kneed knob gobbler	-blowjob (urban)
Knee-deep navy	-epithet for Coast Guard
Knee-deep sailor	-member of Coast Guard
Knee-deep(s)	-belonging to the Coast Guard
Knee dragging	-leaning a motorbike to knee level on a fast curve
Knee ga	-your best buddy (urban)
Knee high to a bumble bee	-small, little, or tiny
Knee high to a French fry	-a small spud
Knee high to a grasshopper	-a tike
Knee high to a milk stool	-short stuff
Knee high to a mosquito	-tiny
Knee high to a splinter	-just a little twig of a thing
Knee high to a toad	-squatty small
Knee jerk liberal	-one with irritating consistently liberal opinions

Knee knockers	-wood and rubber bullets
Knee knockers	-old ladies' saggy breast that knock her knees
Knee-knocker (Navy)	-bulkhead passageway
Knee lift	-wrestling move
Kneepad conservative	-reserved annoying attitudes
Knee shooters (urban)	-droopy breast torpedo tits
Knee toe (urban)	-neato or cool
Kneeball	-Bush's twisted tongue for snowball
Kneebangers (surfer)	-long baggy shorts
Kneebow (urban)	-knee or inside of knee
Kneeeeeeee	-Knights of Kne battle cry
Kneefs (urban)	-the chubby fat that hangs down over knees
Kneepit (urban)	-back side of the knee
Kneepole (urban)	-scabbing or scar on
Kneesie	-martial arts type
Kneet (urban)	-being mentally toasted
Kneevage (urban)	-the roll of excess skin spilling over boots
Kneez (urban)	-sexual insult
Kneez	-exclamation of happiness
Knights of Kne	-Monty Python's goofy crew
Knobs (Blk-American)	-knees
Leg hinge	-knee
Marrow bones (old nautical)	-knees
Marrowbones and cleavers	-music made with ox shin bone & butcher's cleavers
No bigger than a bee's knee	-small
Praying to the porcelain god	-toilet kneeling to vomit
Ruff as a goat's knee	-sandpaper ruff
Spamalot	-Broadway Camelot spoof w/Knights of Kne

AUSSIE:

Bee's knees	-top notch
Knee high to a grasshopper	-very short

BRITISH:

Hayp-knee	-half penny (out of circulation since 1960's)
Kinky boots	-female leather knee boots
Knees-up	-celebration or party

CANADIAN:

Loonies & 2 knees	-Canadian dollar and 2 dollar coin pieces
Knee Dippers	-American political Bush followers

COCKNEY RHYMING (British Cockney Silly Talk):

Bended Knees	-cheese
Biscuits and Cheese	-knees
Chips and Peas	-knees
Dirty knees	-33 in bingo
Hairy Knees	-please
Housemaid's Knees	-seas
Knee-Bender	-religious person
Knee-Trembler	-intercourse standing up
Knobby-Knees	-keys

CORNISH:

As stiff as a barker's knee	-stiff

IRISH:

Deader	-knee someone in the side thigh

SOUTH AFRICAN:

Knee	-no

KNEE VAMPED WORDS

GENERAL:
ACCOMPAN-KNEE
AGON-KNEE
ALAMO-KNEE
AN-KNEE-MAL
ATTURN-KNEE
BALCO-KNEE
BALONE-KNEE
BARN-KNEE-CLE
BEAN-KNEE BABY
BEN-KNEE-FIT
BLAR-KNEE
BONE-KNEE
BONE-KNEE-FIED
BOT-KNEE
BRAIN-KNEE
BRAIN-KNEE-AC
BRAWN-KNEE
BROWN-KNEE
BUN-KNEE
CAN-KNEE-BAL
CAR-KNEE-VAL
CEREMON-KNEE
CHAMPAG-KNEE
CHIMME-KNEE
CHI-KNEES
COLO-KNEE
COMPAN-KNEE
CONE-KNEE
CORN-KNEE
CRAIN-KNEE-UM
CROW-KNEE

DESTI-KNEE
DIN-KNEE-SAUR
FASHION-KNEE-STA
FETACI-KNEE
FUN-KNEE
GENE-KNEE
GOON-KNEE
HARMON-KNEE
HER-KNEE-A
HINE-KNEE
HOM-KNEE
HORN-KNEE
HUN-KNEE
JAPA-KNEES
JOURN-KNEE
KNEE-CE
KNEE-CESSITIES
KNEEDLE
KNEE-DY
KNEESLES
KNEE-ON
LOON-KNEE
MACARONE-KNEE
MAIN-KNEE-AC
MAN-KNEE-KIN
MARTIN-KNEE
MEAN-KNEE
MIN-KNEE MART
MON-KNEE
MOON-KNEE
NOMO-KNEE
PEN-KNEE
PEPPERON-KNEE
PHEW-KNEE

PHONE-KNEE
PO-KNEE
PUN-KNEE
RAIN-KNEE
RUN-KNEE
SPAMON-KNEE
STONE-KNEE
SUN-KNEE
SYPHON-KNEE
TEEN-KNEE
TINE-KNEE
TITAIN-KNEE-UM
TRAIN-KNEE
TOON-KNEE
UNCAN-KNEE
URAIN-KNEE-UM
WEEN-KNEE
WHIN-KNEE

NAMES:
ANN-KNEE
ANTHON-KNEE
BARN-KNEE
BEN-KNEE
BERN-KINEE
BON-KNEE
BRIT-KNEE
BUGS-BUN-KNEE
BUN-KNEE
CLUE-KNEE (George)
CON♥KNEE
COURT-KNEE
CHAIN-KNEE (Dick)
DAN-KNEE
DEN-KNEE

DON-KNEE
FAN-KNEE
HEN-KNEE
HOUDI-KNEE
JEAN-KNEE
JEN-KNEE
JOAN-KNEE
JOHN-KNEE
KEN-KNEE
LEN-KNEE
MAN-KNEE
MIN-KNEE MOUSE
KNEE-O
PEN-KNEE
ROD-KNEE
RON-KNEE
SO-KNEE
SON-KNEE
STEPHEN-KNEE
SYD-KNEE
TOE-KNEE
YAWN-KNEE

PLACES:
ALBAN-KNEE
CONE-KNEE ISLAND
DIZZ-KNEE-LAND
DIZZ-KNEE-WORLD
GERMAN-KNEE
KNEE-BRASKA
KNEE-VADA
SPACE KNEE-DLE
SYD-KNEE

QUOTES

"Have you ever noticed that whatever sport you're trying to learn, some earnest person is always telling you to keep your knees bent?
…Dave Barry

"Yet at my devotion I love to use the civility of my knee, my hat, and hand"
…Thomas Brown, Sr.

"I just think that the knee-jerk reaction to any gun safety measure is wrong."
…Bill Clinton

"Satan trembles when he sees the weakest saint upon their knees"
…William Cowper

"I seated ugliness on my knee, and almost immediately grew tired of it."
…Salvador Dali`

"Ankles are nearly always neat and good-looking but knees are nearly always not."
…Dwight D. Eisenhower

"This a simple question of evolution. The day is quickly coming when every knee shall bow down to a silicon fist, and you will all beg your binary gods for mercy."
…Bill Gates

"Education commences at the mother's knee, and every word spoken within the hearsay of little children tends toward the formation of character."
…Aldous Huxley

"Religion's in the heart, not the knees."
...Douglas William Jerrold

"That best academy, a mother's knee."
...James Russell Lowell

"The only difference between the Republican and Democratic parties is the velocities with which their knees hit the floor when corporations knock on their door. That's the only difference."
...Ralph Nader

Failures are like skinned knees, painful but superficial."
...Ross Perot

SAYINGS

The knee is a device for locating rocks in your garden.
-American

Do you have a Band-Aid? Because I just scraped my knee falling for you!
-American

Corn should be 'knee high by the 4th of July'.
-American

A piece on incense may be as large as the knee, but unless burnt remits no fragrance.
-Malayan

The heart is not a knee, it does not bend.
-Togo

KNEECHÉS

Here all roads lead to Knee and this writer came up with over fifty pages of these cliché chestnuts. However, less is better so taking one's own advice they will be kept to a minimum.

A KNEE IS A KNEE IS A KNEE.
A MAN PASSES FOR WHAT KNEEZ WORTH.
A WAIT AND KNEE ATTITUDE-
AIN'T KNEE SWEET-
ALL YOU KNEED IS LOVE.
AS I LAY KNEE DOWN TO SLEEP-
ASK KNEE NO QUESTIONS, I'LL TELL YOU NO LIES.
ASS OVER KNEE KETTLE-
ATTACK OF THE KILLER KNEES-
BACK KNEE UP-
BE ALL THAT YOU CAN KNEE.
BEAM KNEE UP SCOTTY.
BEAT KNEE WITH A STICK.
BEAUTY IS ONLY KNEE DEEP.
BELIEVE IN KNEE.
BEND KNEE, SHAKE KNEE-
BETTER YOU THAN KNEE-
BITE KNEE-
BLOOD MON-KNEE-
BLOW KNEE OVER-
BLUE MEAN-KNEES-
BORN KNEE-
BROW-KNEE POINTS-
BUSY AS A KNEE-
BUZZ KNEE-
CALL KNEE CRAZY.
CALL KNEE IRESISTABLE.
CAN'T BUY KNEE LOVE-

CAN'T KNEE ALL JUST GET ALONG?
CAN'T SEE THE FOREST THROUGH THE KNEES-
CAR-KNEEVAL ATMOSPHERE-
CATCH KNEE IF YOU CAN-
CHARM THE BIRDS OUT OF THE KNEES.
CLUE KNEE IN-
COFFEE, TEA OR KNEE-
COLD KNEES WARM HEART-
COUNT KNEE IN-
COUNT KNEE OUT-
CROSS YOUR KNEE AND HOPE TO DIE-
CRY KNEE A RIVER.
DARE TO BE KNEE.
DEAL KNEE IN.
DIARY OF A SKINNED KNEE-
DO THE LOCAMOTION WITH KNEE.
DO YOU WANT A PIECE OF KNEE?
DOE, RAE, KNEE, FA, SO, LA TE-
DOG AND PO-KNEE SHOW-
DON'T WORRY KNEE HAPPY.
FAR BE IT FROM KNEE.
FOOL ME ONCE SHAME ON KNEE.
FOOT LOOSE AND FANCY KNEE-
FUN-KNEE, VERY FUN-KNEE-
GET RELIGION, BEND A KNEE.
GIVE KNEES A CHANCE.
GOT KNEE?
HAVE KNEES WILL TRAVEL.
HE LOVES KNEE, HE LOVES KNEE NOT.
HEAR NO EVIL, SPEAK NO EVIL, KNEE NO EVIL.
HEY, LOOK KNEE OVER.
HIT KNEE WITH YOUR BEST SHOT.
HOLD KNEE TIGHT.
HON-KNEE DO LIST-

HOOK KNEE UP.
HOUR OF KNEED.
HOUSTON, KNEE HAVE A PROBLEM.
HUN-KNEE PIE-
I DREAM OF GEN-KNEE.
I KNEE LONDON, I KNEE FRANCE.
I'M PROUD TO KNEE AN AMERICAN.
IF YOU CAN KNEE ME, YOU'RE TOO CLOSE.
IF YOU SHOW KNEE YOURS, I'LL SHOW YOU MINE.
IN THE KNEE HOURS-
IT BEATS KNEE.
IT SHOULD HAVE BEEN KNEE.
IT'S ALL GREEK TO KNEE.
IT'S BEYOND KNEE.
JOHN-KNEE COME LATELY.
JUST KNEE AND MY SHADOW-
KEEPING KNEE ON PINS AND KNEEDLES-
KISS KNEE QUICK.
KNEE AFRAID, KNEE VERY AFRAID-
KNEE ALL THAT YOU CAN KNEE-
KNEE AND CRUMPETS-
KNEE AND MY BABY, MY BABY AND KNEE-
KNEE ARE FAMILY-
KNEE AS A BIRD-
KNEE DEEP IN WONDER-
KNEE FOR TWO-
KNEE FOR YOU AND YOU FOR KNEE-
KNEE SHALL OVERCOME.
KNEE STRIKES AND YOU'RE OUT.
KNEE THAT AS IT MAY.
KNEE THE PEOPLE.
KNEE THERE OR KNEE SQUARE.
KNEE WILL ROCK YOU.
KNEE, MYSELF AND I.-

KNEED BETWEEN THE LINES-
KNEED IS THE MOTHER OF INVENTION.
KNEED THEM AND REAP.
KNEEDS SUPERVISION-
KNEEL TO HEAL.
KNEE-NER, KNEE-NER, KNEE-NER-
KNEET AND TIDY-
KNEEZ AND THANK YOU-
KNOCK KNEE OVER WITH A FEATHER.
LET IT KNEE.
LET KNEE ENTERTAIN YOU.
LIE, CHEAT AND KNEEL.
LONG TIME NO KNEE.
LOVE KNEE OR LEAVE KNEE.
MERCY KNEE!
MISERY LOVES COMPAN-KNEE-
MISSED KNEE, NOW YOU HAVE TO KISS KNEE-
MOM LIKES KNEE BEST.
MONEY DOES'NT GROW ON KNEES.
MONKEY KNEE, MONKEY DO.
NEVER A LENDER OR BORROWER KNEE-
NOT FOR ALL THE KNEE IN CHINA.
NOT MY CUP OF KNEE.
ON A KNEED TO KNOW BASIS.
ON THE SUN-KNEE SIDE OF THE STREET-
ONE GOOD KNEED DESERVES ANOTHER.
ONETH BY COUNTRY, TWOETH BY KNEE.
PEN-KNEES FROM HEAVEN-
PO-KNEE UP-
PROUD TO BE KNEE-
ROCK ABY BABY IN THE KNEE TOP-
RUN KNEE RAGGED-
SAY A LITTLE PRAYER FOR KNEE-
SENTIMENTAL JOUR-KNEE-

SHIVER KNEE TIMBERS-
SHOOTING THE KNEEZ-
SOCK IT TO KNEE.
SOMEONE TO WATCH OVER KNEE-
SOMETIMES A KNEE IS JUST A KNEE.
SPARE KNEE THE DETAILS.
STAND BY KNEE.
STILL WATERS RUN KNEE DEEP-
SUN-KNEE DISPOSITION-
TAKE KNEE OUT TO THE BALL GAME.
TAKE KNEE TO THE RIVER.
TAKE KNEE TO YOUR LEADER.
TAKE THE MON-KNEE AND RUN.
TELL KNEE, TELL KNEE, TELL KNEE TRUE-
THAT WILL KNEE THE DAY.
THE BEST THINGS IN LIFE ARE KNEE.
THE POWERS THAT KNEE-
THEY'RE COMING TO TAKE KNEE AWAY-HA HA
TICKLE MY FUN-KNEE BONE.
TO KNEE OR NOT TO KNEE-
TO YOUR OWN SELF KNEE TRUE.
TROPICAL KNEEZ-
TWO'S COMPAN-KNEE, KNEES A CROWD-
WAY OUT IN THE BOON-KNEES.
WHAT IS THIS A KNEE PARTY?
WHO KNEED IN YOUR CORNFLAKES?
WHY KNEE, WHY ALWAYS KNEE?
YOU AND KNEE AGAINST THE WORLD-
YOU KNOCK KNEE OUT.
YOU SWEPT KNEE OFF MY FEET.
YOU'RE BARKING UP THE WRONG KNEE.
YOU'VE REALLY GOT A HOLD ON KNEE.

WARNING: excessive use may incite a knee-a-thon or
            an overwhelming bout of giggles.

SYMBOLISM

Echoing from the dawn of being spectacular origin myths has delivered moral, social and emotional directives with symbols. These are primarily ideas portrayed by man-made figurative images. Technically all concepts are representative in design. Capable of conveying meanings with pictures allows involvement of thought and quantity. They may be literal (but not necessarily exact) or own an additional dimension of mystic. Their pervasive prints are the components of life's cadence.

Knees with their varied affiliations exhibit instrumental patterns in setting the pace of vitality and initiating compelling themes.

Finish allegoric narratives speak about the mother of water, virgin of air. With her knee risen from the sea a Goldeneye gracefully nested on top. One steel and six golden eggs were laid. As they brooded for several days, the knee became scorched and it made her flinch. This caused the heated eggs to spill out to cold ocean waves. The shock cracked them to pieces that then turned into all things rare and beautiful.

For North American Choctaw Indians the creator began by forming a great mound called Nanih Wiya. Crawling through long dark caverns from this abyss, they believed themselves to be first of the peoples to emerge into the light.

Celts contend Brighde, goddess of the land as an innovated force. She and her counter parts transcended into Christianity as 'knee-woman' to Mary and foster mother to Jesus.

Egyptians ascribed to numerous stories. Some perceived that with his knee bent to the skies Geb, Earth God, modeled the mountains and valleys. An ideogram of a knee (knee-bend-slope) ⌐ is still visible in one of the oldest of their temples.

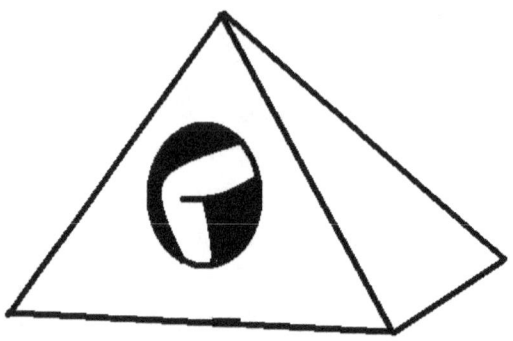

The 'primal hill' is a hieroglyphic that also exemplifies an understanding of beginnings. From chaotic seas, a mound of earth erupted into dry land. Its' profound resonating effects show up in temple layouts, pyramids, and the cosmic mast. Hindus identified these steps with a crescent ship to the celestial mountain. Aztecs had climbing the ladder of redemption. All seen as ascension, stages or layers and the count of steps (or runs) forge number factors. A majority insinuate stairways to heaven, vertical bridges leading to perfection, roadways to gods plus a bond between earth and divinity.

(Mast=bridge=ladder=steps=knee=slope=hill=mound=oreo (Greek for hill mound) =Oreo cookie=Oreo cookie for me!)

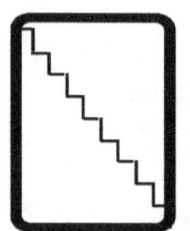 Gypsy made mention of a nascent Egyptian padding for protection of knees tagged the 'Khet Patch'. Generally, it was made of leather that was boiled so it could be molded and tooled. They were secured with straps that wrapped or tied behind the knee, embellished with an emblem of a staircase, representing steps as well as bending of the knee. Furthermore during life the body was referred to khet meaning appearance or otherwise a ship's mast.

Khet is an Egyptian measurement equivalent to 1/10 of minute of degree=350 royal cubits=183.4519 meters=.11399176 miles=200.625 yards

In the Himalayan Mountains, khet is a type of wet terraced farming. Slanted steps are carved into the grade and reinforced by small rock walls. Supported by an irrigation system they have a high rate of productivity of rice and wheat growth.

Panjabi and Urdu both have khet expressions that have the English translation of field. With Yiddish, it's defined as sin while in Hebrew it is fence and the eighth letter of their alphabet.

TRISKELION (Greek for 'three-legged') is apparent in several cultures representing progress, competition, stability or possibly a trinity of deities.

Norse legends introduced a three-pronged solar spiral emulating sun movement of running through the heavens. Celtic and Hopi Indians had similar simple geometric designs. Contemporary usage includes a right wing South African organization 〰 with the lines running in a counter clockwise rotation; serving as a group logo it represents desire to 'put the clock back'. The figure ⊘ signifies a type of winding for an electrical transformer. Power begets power!

Greek legs have been found in prehistoric rock carvings of northern Italy plus on a trophy shield, coins and vases from the 6th to 8th centuries BC, assimilating eternal movement.

Sicilian flag renditions have a monstrous mask or medusa face in the center of the conjoined bare knees, occasionally garnished with foliage, snakes or wings.

In Isle of Man adaptations, the legs are armored and surfaced around 1300.

It's not only on their flag but on the coat of arms as well. Under scored with the motto 'Quocunque Jeceris Stabit'- 'whithersoever you throw it, it will stand'. Strong words speak for themselves.

Sacred needlework in clothing was a common with witchcraft and its' offspring. There are religious versions that have lasted into the present. Cassocks of Ukrainian Christian priests have 45° diamonds embroidered backside at knee level. Called kustodia (custody) and depicting sheltering while simultaneously professing the crucifixion. Mormons have gleaned their holy garb from Freemasons since the mid 1800 hundreds. A mark of horizontal lines is stitched over the right knee of their private under garments. The purpose being a daily reminder that every knee shall bow and every tongue confess Jesus is the savior.

Showing off wealth or accomplishments on the head has always occurred. Clout in the Stone Age was flaunting tibias of respected elders or defeated enemies. One of the easiest recognizable caricatures is an over exaggerated cartoon cavewoman with a shinbone knotted in her hair.

The 'skull and crossbones' is an icon consisting of a human skull resting atop two crossed bones (femur or tibia, those are knee bones folks!). Yale University's elite secret society is 'Skull and Bones'. Freemasons recognized 'skull and crossbones' as an insignia of the fleetingness of material existence, they were used in initiations representing spiritual revival. It may also have presence in the kabalistic 'Tree of Life' (a doorway to higher wisdom), which is only accomplished by the death and rebirth of one's conscious soul.

Best known as the 'Jolly Roger' and identified with buccaneers. Supposedly, it was friendly merchant vessels that originally sported red marked flags. The French referred to them as 'joli rouge' meaning 'pretty red'. It was believed tricky traders took advantage of the welcoming atmosphere and betrayed by looting. The title then was said to snidely reflect sight of the bloodthirsty classic pirate motif (white on black) which instilled fears of ruthless pillaging, no man left alive, walking the plank, and all sorts of skullduggery. Here's where historical waters get murky-a second thought was it came from 'Old Roger', a byname for the devil. Yet another that it was copied from an image captains would record in their ship's log when a sailor died. The 'Death' head still evokes warnings of danger, labeling containers of poison, toxic chemicals and explosives.

Mathematic 'Greater Than' Symbol:
BIG > small

> The value on the left is larger than value on right.

< Denotes value on left is smaller the value on right.

≤ Indicates value on left is smaller than or equal to value on right.

≥ Value on left is larger than or equal value on right.

Knees have a long-standing legato (direction) in the universal language of music providing visual cues for structuring sound levels.

> Diminuendo-a decrease in volume

< Crescendo-an increase in volume

Check out your stereo or any recording equipment ironically the control signs directing degrees of loudness are reversed.

▶ Crank it up

◀ Turn it down

USA race walking officials use paddles to flag warnings during competitions. One side depicts bending of the knee > (a serious no-no in speed walking). Three such infractions can constitute disqualification.

All of these knee reflections have a rhythm that runs consistent with their functional and spiritual forms. It's fascinating how their commonalities surpassed the rat race.

TATTOOS-

In 1991, Ozti the Ice Man, oldest tattooed body known was discovered in the Alps between Austria and Italy. The mummified Bronze Age hunter dating back 5300 years was so well preserved researchers were able to distinguish numerous hued glyph images. Included in these was a cross, situated inside of the left knee. Scientific speculation suggests their locations had therapeutic applications possibly related to acupuncture points. The actual meanings remain a puzzle.

Artic pigment marks, specifically on St. Lawrence Island, go back over 2000 years. This was a settlement of seafaring people weathering an isolated environment and governed by an animistic religion. Subcutaneous funeral dye stains became an important tool to atone the temperaments of these gods. After death it was perceived a deceased person's negative "shade" lingered awhile seeking refuge in another being by attacking the most vulnerable entry points (joints-such as knees). Because of close contact, pallbearers took great preventive pains by having a large bone needle with whale sinew (soaked in a concoction of urine, seal oil, and scrapings of lampblack) pierced through their epidermis. This process was in one side then out the other leaving two "dots" to protect and block these juncture portals. This method was also used in their "first kill" tributes in respect of the animals' sacrifice and to repel any evil entities.

Initially outsiders mistook Samoans as wearing artful close fitting silk breeches, in actuality they were adorned with elaborate flesh scarifications from mid-torso to just below the knees. For two thousand years, pubescent island boys would follow their ancestors into this unbroken tradition. This is an intricate process involving hand tapping the skin with a small hammer and inked teeth of a boar comb. Mind you, the practice was neither pleasant nor easy.

Even the intimate areas were not ignored and any crying only resulted in cruel taunting. Completion could take up to three months and then a year to heal. This intense and painful experience harbored a rite of passage into manhood by showing their strength, bravery and dedication. Female participants underwent lacier coverings from upper thighs to diamonds behind the knees. Densely patterned ribbons about the width of a hand decorated backsides of male knees. Although it is no longer a prerequisite to enter adulthood, their culture still supports and honors this style as body beautification.

Naga is a region in northeastern India, of its' many groups is the Konjak tribe. Female members rejoice in the monumental stages of their lives with permanent skin symbols. Marital status is merited and acknowledged with a tat behind the knee.

Continued exploration across briny deep waters broadened the horizons and popularity of tattoos. Aside from visual mementos of their voyages, there were maritime superstition pigmentations. A porker on one knee and a cock on the other was good luck or a precaution from starvation: by always carrying their own "ham and eggs" with them. Whereas Canadian sailors with a swine above their shin do so as a protection from drowning, this is according to the rhyme "Pig on the knee safety at sea."

There are instances where knee tattooing has been encouraged for relief of arthritic discomfort. Condensed needle pricking brings blood to the surface and stimulates healthy circulation.

KNEES AT LARGE

Infamous Hall of Flame

1890- 'MASSACRE AT WOUNDED KNEE'
A period of treaties and cultural clashes thought
as one of the most disturbing episodes in U.S.
history. White government officials had banned
Sioux from observing their spiritual rites, when
they continued military control took over the
situation. Without resistance Ghost Dancers and
reservation renegades were corralled to wait for
troops along the wintry banks of Wounded
Knee Creek, South Dakota. The Calvary road
in to save the day, confiscate guns and organize
relocation. Instead, something went terribly
awry resulting in a horrifying bloodbath of
approximately 300 presumably innocent men,
women and children. Acknowledged as last
major armed 'battle' and a means to an end for
the century long American-Indian Wars.
(Notably accounts differ.)

1939- 'ELSIE OF THE DIMPLED KNEES'
Miss Crabtree was University of Nevada's lead
majorette. Dean of Women decided outfits
were too revealing and encouraged unladylike
routines. She decreed the girl's six inches above
the knee skirts would have to be lengthened to
one inch below. This caused such a fuss it
became a nationally newsworthy topic. Elsie's
popular knobs traveled about the countryside
strutting their stuff at various events. An
invitation to perform in Hollywood's season
opener 'Candy Cane Lane' was the final

downfall. Threats to boycott festivities if those outlandish knees participated abated the phenomenon.

1956- 'ELVIS'S KNEE SHAKE'

September 9th was Presley's springboard début on the Ed Sullivan TV Variety Hour. Over four-fifths of the country's viewing audience was captivated. Shocking while rocking them with raw suggestive gyrations and his signature shut down knee shake shimmy. Mercy! By his last performance on June 6, 1957, he had dyed his hair 'bad boy' jet black and the show was concerned about rumors that other attributes may be enhanced. To protect their wholesome image and prevent igniting sexually charged teenage fans the King was filmed from his waist up.

1970- 'CLAIRE'S KNEE'

This is the fifth film in a series of six 'Moral Tales' by Eric Rohmer. The award winning French cinema's masterpiece is the provocative story of a man's classic internal struggle with hidden desire and temptation. An engaged career diplomat's holiday acquaintance with a younger female evokes a strangely obscure obsession, Claire's knee. His first vision of her intoxicating knee-while she's upon a ladder picking ripe cherries is considered an iconic image for the intriguing collection.

1986- 'OLYMPIC KNEE BASHING'

During U.S. Figure Skating Championships there was an attempt to maim thus remove contender Nancy Kerrigan from competition. Controversy surrounded rival teammate Tonya Harding's involvement. It was her husband and cohorts charged with the brutal knee clubbing. Kerrigan recovered and went on to become the Silver Medalist.

1995- 'PRESIDENTIAL KNEE PADS"
A phrase and product generated by a scandalous relationship in Clinton's first term. Allegedly, Monica Lewinsky had made a comment of "I'm going to Washington D.C. to earn my presidential knee pads." Her intended route was an internship in the White House. Later at great expense to Americans, the tawdry affair was exposed involving; taped telephone conversations, affidavits, grand jury testimony, indictments, and an impeachment hearing. Lewinsky's statement resurfaced in a political frenzy, media fed it to nightly talk show hosts and comedians who brought the term mainstream. Subsequently web entrepreneurs developed funny styles of Commander & Chief Knee Pads as gag gifts or risqué souvenirs.

END CREDITS;

The Association of International Karma Police certifies monitored knee(s) action. In compliance be assured no knee(s) have been harmed, mistreated, manhandled or abused during the research and development of this double-jointed publication.

R ESOURCES:

The World Wide Web including copyright free graphics-

Gray's Anatomy of the Human Body-1918
  by Henry Gray

Gypsy's Basic Knee Reader-1974
  by Gypsy Rose Knee

The Land of Osiris-2001
  by Stephen S. Mehler